Skoob Books Publishing Ltd., Lo

Skoob *PACIFICA* is contributi
English, disseminating regional l
and promoting understanding betw

At the turn of the last century, Europe developed a penchant for novels set in lands afar which had a tendency to look **at** the colonies whereas the Postcolonials view from within themselves, experimenting with the deviation from tradition and affirming the aesthetic of the sublime as against an aesthetic of the beautiful.

"The reality of cultural entity should be the simultaneous act of eliciting from history, mythology, and literature, for the benefit of both genuine aliens and the alienated, a continuing process of self-apprehension whose temporary dislocation appears to have persuaded many of its non-existence or its irrelevance (= retrogression, reactionarism, racism, etc.) in contemporary world reality."

Wole Soyinka, *Nobel Laureate*

"Storytelling, to the readers of a *genre* of novel, written by a particular writer for a small group of people in a large and fragmented culture, still survives in those places the English like to call the Commonwealth. This idea of narration, of the active voice is in the calypsonian as the ballad singer, the narrator, the political satirist."

Derek Walcott, *Nobel Laureate*

As the *fin-de-millenium* approaches, the colonies have a voice of their own, a new *genre* has developed. Ironically, this diachrony is written in the language of the Imperialist. Behind the facade of tropical, sandy beaches and factories of video games lies the cross-cultural and interliterary tradition of two continents.

Skoob *PACIFICA: THE EMPIRE WRITES BACK !*

SKOOB *Pacifica* SERIES

Joint Series Editors: Ms. C.Y. Loh & Mr. I.K. Ong

SKOOB *Pacifica* SERIES

No. 2002

WAYS OF EXILE
Poems from the First Decade

By the same author:

Poetry
How the Hills Are Distant (1968)
Remembering Grandma and Other Rumours (1989)

Wong Phui Nam

WAYS OF EXILE
Poems from the First Decade

Foreword

by

K.S. Maniam

English Department
University of Malaya, Kuala Lumpur

Afterword

by

Professor Alan Durant

School of English, Cultural & Communication Studies
Middlesex University, London

SKOOB BOOKS PUBLISHING
LONDON

First published in 1993 by
SKOOB BOOKS PUBLISHING LTD.
Skoob *PACIFICA* Series
11A-17 Sicilian Avenue
off Southampton Row and
Bloomsbury Square
London WC1a 2QH
Fax: 71-404 4398

ISBN 1-871438-09-8

Agents:
Skoob Books (Malaysia) Sdn Bhd.
11 Jalan Telawi Tiga, Bangsar Baru,
59100 Kuala Lumpur
Tel/Fax: 603-255 2686

Graham Brash (Pte) Ltd.
32 Gul Drive
Singapore 2262
Tel: 65-861 1336, 65-862 0437
Fax: 65-861 4815

Typeset by Pearly Kok . Tel/Fax: 603-255 2686
Printed by Polygraphic, Malaysia. Fax: 603-905 1553

IT IS ILLEGAL TO PHOTOCOPY !

For
my wife Khatijah
and my children
Sha'arin, Nor Azah, Rizal and Qushairi

Contents

FOREWORD

By
K.S. MANIAM
English Department
University of Malaya
Kuala Lumpur

In Wong Phui Nam's poetry there is a recurring reference to light and, often enough, to darkness. But it is the imagery centred on light and brightness that finally gains ascendency. One comes across lines such as 'you slipped into the plunging bright arc of your descent' or 'And then...a new daybreak' or 'to think of the splendour of the breaking light at dawn'. These lines and the cluster of similarly veined images encapsulate for the reader not a world lighted up completely but a world awaiting discovery.

This is the persistent note of expectation that runs through the collection: the need to discover. A close reading of Phui Nam's poems makes one realize that this persistence is not centred on some immediate need to extract the epiphanic from a particular, ordinary experience. The many and various linkages and inter-connections between the poems themselves suggest the contrary. Behind the "I" in the poems there is a questing, probing cons-ciousness that has grown from a self seeing itself in a relationship with its surroundings to one that sees itself as a part of a larger, human continuum.

While this is true of poetry written in any time and in any part of the world, the social, cultural and political situations in Malaysia make different and arduous demands on the writer. In addition there is that complex linguistic ocean to cross and make one's own, especially when the writer uses English - not his mother tongue - in his works. This is not so apparent in these postcolonial times when some of the leading literary figures in Britain and France are from the former colonies. It is more than apparent now that English is a global literary language. Writers from Africa, India and the West Indies have amply driven this point home. The struggle of Malaysian writers, however, to reach the point of no return in terms of linguistic choice is hardly known or only remotely understood.

In examining Phui Nam's development as a poet, I am not approaching him merely as a poet but as a poet who has had to reach his present achievement through a persistent struggle with language and cultural perceptions. This is where the history and social structure of a country helps or hinders a writer. In a country where linguistic and literary traditions are established and often work together, the writer is able to assert his distinct, imaginative personality by rebelling against those very traditions. But what happens to a writer who resides in a country where the social structure is rigid and literary traditions nebulous?

These were the conditions under which Phui Nam wrote the poems in this collection, from the 1960's to the early 1970's. The social structure was indeed rigid in that - and continues to be so - it worked on a communal basis. The Malays, Chinese, Indians and Eurasians lived side by side, emphasizing communal territoriality; there was hardly any cross-over into other cultures and if there were, these were individual, isolated events. This meant that the various communities were loyal to their own languages and the cultures that accompanied them.

The writer using English in his works found himself in a dilemma. Could he use the language in the form he inherited it from his British colonisers? If he did he would not only be doing what others around him were doing, he would also be undermining his own role as a poet. A poet is a transformer, not a follower. A poet trans-forms, that is, he reaches into that centre from which he feels all life - individual human beings as well as cultures - comes. For him, this involves the process of unveiling or reinstating shapes, colours, thoughts, feelings and societies as they would have come from the original creative fires.

In the political, social and cultural contexts this would mean unmasking the false, decrying the hypocritical, denouncing the despotic. But above all, he attempts to remove, if only by eroding attitudes and prejudices, the schisms caused by communal loyalties, political power bickering and cultural dogmatism. He counterpoints the present, hollow living with a vision of man and society living under a sky of larger myths, in dignity.

All this implies that language cannot be used in any inherited sense. Phui Nam recognized this when in his introduction to the first edition of *How the Hills are Distant* (1968): "On looking back I realise I have written these poems for those who truly understand what it means to make one's language as one goes along." The poems in this collection testify to that recognition: the language does not merely function as a medium that carries with it all the associations it has accumulated through the years in another country. While the basic meanings of words may be retained, the poet has had to infuse newer significances that more than adequately reflects his own cultural outlook and values.

The four sections in this collection, *How the Hills are Distant, For a Local Osiris, What Are the Roots...*, *Rumours of Exits*, therefore, chart Phui Nam's attempts in the first decade of his poetic career to make language serve rather than to serve that language. He makes the language enact the experience of living in Malaysia, with all the attendant preoccupations of questioning the lives and attitudes of the people, his own place in that society and - not putting aside the feeling of expectation - images that kind of individual and society that can emerge from a multinational setting.

The *Hills* cycle of poems examines the poet's relationship with the peoples, cultures and politics of the country. He seeks, through them, an identity with the cultural and historical past of the multiracial society in which he lives. To this complexity he brings his own cultural inheritance, namely, that of the Chinese tradition, that residue of memory originating in China and reaching him through the line of predecessors who formed the first five generations of settlers in Malaysia.

The main support of the series comes from the landscape that represents simultaneously the physical lay-out of the country, the social environment and his interior consciousness. The landscape, recording the archetypal memory of man, evolves from a natural, rural environment, shaped by the elements, through to the urban, moulded by man. Phui Nam develops an imagery that originating in the pristine, intuitive nature of man, reaches through to the urban, rational sensibility of modern man. The language, as does the style, gradually discards the old, mythic features in order to reflect man's present intellectual approach to life and a consciousness that relies less on a spontaneous surrender to the emotions.

For a Local Osiris represents a confrontation with himself. It is a psychological recognition of his personality, leading finally to the birth of an aesthetic and spiritual self. *Osiris* takes his psyche to the precipice so that the poet can know the limits of his present consciousness and, subsequently, enter a new one. The theme and connecting thread in all these poems is death. There is the death of meaning, emotion, courage, the spirit and the intellect. The landscape here is interiorized and becomes the landscape of an inner consciousness or soul. As in the Osiris myth each of the poems represents a part of the poet's present psyche that must be killed and buried before a wholesome rebirth can occur. The tone in each of the poems is that of steady confrontation leading to recognition and then acceptance. Taken together they define the cyclic nature of man's emotional, intellectual and spiritual selves. With this recognition he is compelled to make, more consciously, a world-view that keeps pace with his developing consciousness. The poems in this section "Osiris Transmogrified" and "Address from the God" counterpoint the descent into despair with the positive, life-giving desire to create, for oneself at least, a more complex and inclusive consciousness.

The sections that follow, *What are the Roots...* and *Rumours of Exits*, logically move into concerns that transcend personal preoccupations. *Roots* represents a return to his Chinese origins but not as to a nostalgic cultural celebration. It is more like a reshaping of the experiences presented by Tu Fu in his works and by eight Taoist poems, to highlight just two of the subsections. They are translations, though not literal ones, and the poet's choice of these particular poems remark on the development that comes after *Hills* and *Osiris*. In these works, it would appear that Phui Nam is engaged in linking two different times and land-scapes to suggest the universality of man's recognitions and longings. These lines from "In the North": 'Where convulsions of the times have gouged/ from the land farms, markets, fields and cities,/ there can be no more hope of word from home' contain the realization that wars, those man-made disasters, would continue throughout the history of mankind. The word 'home' creates the poignant recognition that there can never be a home, only a longing for it.

As a sense of liberation comes through in these recreated poems. In "Summer in the Foothills" the poet says:

> This is a summer that smoulders in the flesh.
> So, with all my clothes, I cast away my fan
> and lie there naked, deep in these dense, green woods.
> Up on that rock-face my girdle dangles in the sun.
> The wind comes whistling from the mountain pines
> and bathes my head in wide, cool and dreamless spaces.

The liberation comes from his discarding the cultural outfits he has been trying to get into and not quite succeeding. His nature is not to be trapped within a particular, zenophobic cultural encasing. In a multiracial society virtue can be made of the practice of extolling the qualities of one's own culture against that of others. The poet recognizes the danger in this attitude: it could lead to an intolerant, narrow-minded smugness. These creative translations are therefore the poet's way of unfolding what I can only, for want of a better term, call the more fulfilling process of inhabitation.

This process of inhabitation is tied to the expectation of discovery, mentioned at the beginning of this introduction. While this can be treated merely as a literary activity, it can be more fruitfully viewed as a practical need for the individual in a multiracial society to leave behind the self shaped by his own cultural milieu and enter the self of a personality formed by another culture or cultures. Through the use of inhabitation, Phui Nam makes an ironic comment on one's roots. The roots one sees as one's cultural history proves to be the opposite: one's own cultural history is merely a passing expression of one's social existence. The real roots lie beyond the cultural and social traditions man has evolved for himself. They lie in that region of the original life-force and the force of the imagination.

In-habitation is the process of continually entering, immersing in and emerging from one form of culture/existence and then entering through the same process another form of culture/ existence. The section, *Rumours of Exits*, demonstrates the workings of this process. "A Death in the Ward" details a Chinese boy's entry into the mind/mindlessness of Manickam, an Indian, The images here function to reveal both the boy's and the Indian's aborted lives - so that the reader is emotionally compelled to equate the boy's life with the old man's.

Exits, ironically, is not concerned with escape; it is more preoccupied with departures. These departures are a going away from self-locking outlooks and attitudes, into forms of awareness that continually enlarge one's personality. Thus the subsections "From Chairil Anwar", "Temple Caves" and "A Night Easter" are such departures. Through these departures the poet continues to extend not only his awareness but also his capacity to feel and to imagine. The last two allow him to enter other cultures and, briefly, make them his own. "From Chairil Anwar" captures the personality of an individual in revolt against a constricting social environment and against individuals who think and feel in limited ways. Phui Nam manages to break into the Indonesian poet's bold intimacies and the abrasive but delightful bringing down of conservative attitudes and attachments.

"Temple Caves" goes deeper into the spiritual awareness of man than *Hills* and *Osiris* do. In this series of poems one enters into the agony of the man, the 'being of the senses', who is unable to discover the proper expressions for his spirituality:

> All that we can hope to know about being more
> than merely human is held fast, mixed in with coarse grain
> in bodies, calcified into substance
> that daily becomes more solid, more resistant than stone.

Yet this recognition in itself is a discovery; his awareness of the more than the human is expressed through the pain of being only bodily human.

The anxiety and uncertainty about one's spiritual nature does not trail off into a contemplation of the void; that would be a surrender to a hopeless and unwarranted despair. Could not the mystery that surrounds the spiritual origins of man be celebrated in a realistic manner and in surroundings the most mundane? Phui Nam demonstrates in "A Night Easter" that this is not only possible but necessary. This poem, while referring to Christ's resurrection, dramatises the Christ or the god-head in any ordinary man. Through the voices that speak, mourn and recall an unnamed man's violent death in the estate lines, the poem raises that ordinary man's demise to the level of Christ's crucifixion. This is done not just to strain at parallels but rather to give spiritual value to any man who passes through this world. More than that, it evokes, once again, for us the feeling that every life comes from the god-head and therefore is the god-head.

Ways of Exile, as a collection, embraces various concerns to all of which this introduction cannot give the attention. They deserve what is obvious, however, is that here is an effulgent intelligence that tries to find for itself a meaningful place in a multiracial society. In doing so it has always avoided the parochial and from the earliest poems has tried to place the poet's Malaysian experience within a universal, human paradigm. The poet has had to weave his way through his own culture, of which he can hardly be sure, and through the cultures of the other races in the country. The collection, as a whole, demonstrates that the concepts about culture, history and language have to be re-examined so that broader human and spiritual expressions of these aspects of man's existence can be discovered.

Skoob *Pacifica* gratefully acknowledge the cooperation of *The New Straits Times* for their permission to publish the following works:
Readings from Tu Fu ii, iii, iv, vi, vii & viii;
Taoist Poems i, ii, iii, v, vi, vii, & viii;
Reading of a Tang Poem and Postscript - Out of the Stony Rubbish.

I

How the Hills Are Distant

INTRODUCTION
to
How the Hills Are Distant

These poems were to have been published as a collection in 1963. The publishing trade being what it is in this country, the book never quite made it. Most of the poems were published as part of an anthology of Malaysian writing, *Bunga Emas*.

Poor business aside, for our publishers verse in English is really a matter of courage. At the heart of it must be the anxiety that it is difficult to justify the claims of poems such as these on even the language in which they are written. But these poems need to be written. They are of a time, of a place, of a people who find themselves having to live by institutions and folkways which are not of their heritage, having to absorb the manners of languages not their own. Such little knowledge as comes to them of the human predicament is no less knowledge than what comes to other peoples in other times and places.

These poems will always have to suffer the misunderstanding of anthologists and translators with ample trust funds, who sleep untroubled on assumptions that the only valid Asian or African poetry must be poetry in the "native" languages; the misunderstanding of English critics who can read verse only in terms of what is happening in present day England. Poems in English do not necessarily have to be English poetry. The tradition lays down the ground rules as to how the language is to be used. But its assumptions about the image of man to himself, about his relationship to the State, God and the physical universe must be the beginnings of our difficulties. These are the received assumptions, yet we cannot affect with them the ease and familiarity of a true inheritance.

On looking back I realise I have written these poems for those who truly understand what it means to have to make one's language as one goes along.

Wong Phui Nam

How the Hills Are Distant

i

When I am dead
and the old man, the river,
after a night of rain among the hills
should come upon me,
I shall only stir
like stones that drag the muddy bed.

When I am dead
should the old man rage
and relieve himself upon the fields,
my heart shall no more
be taut with kneading
that works from silt, green tumescent heads.

The old man grows,
lives from subconscious hills,
sentient in fishes and reeds that slant
towards eloquence of words.
The waterfowl cry
his flowering of vowels on the wind.

If like you, old man,
I should never die
but learn my way about the hills,
I should be glad
always of rain
till the bunds of my body break and are washed in sand.

ii

With such violence as shattered walls of rain
when the sky's torpor broke, heavy for its slate,
the storm drags up a broken afternoon
of cowed trees and houses, and from the fields
the mud invades our doorsteps. The light slants,
splayed against the tree-tops of the old estate
and some of the trees put out tentative boughs of glory.
At the hill-top the house stands, with shadows
etching their intents across its bare faces
touching upon fringes, only of ambiguities.
The afternoon brightens, the heart, sudden upon urge
of swallows against the sky. In full flowering by the gate
the crinum lilies fountain inconclusive into the after-light
when I withdraw to be indoors, the heart to be within the body's house.

iii

The mist drifting across the field
edges up the compound of my house,
along the foot of the hibiscus hedge
moving vaguely like fear among the cane.

I sit up to watch, as I have on many nights
from my darkness at the window,
my heart precise within these walls,
my room with its table and rumpled bed.

It is imminent; in the sudden smell
of wet grass and stir among the frangipani,
in the straight tensed fence-posts in half-light

against the margin of encroaching sleep
where I anticipate only, a waking
to vague remembrance of a harrowing in my dream.

iv

In the red light of an afternoon
gathered on the goldfish in the garden
where edges break in the bond of things
shadows harden, confuse with their plantain leaves.

In the stillness of the ear-drum
the tractor gashes its way up the hill
of stone structures deposited of time and flexed muscles,
pounding the tom-tom of the drums:

tessellated in the liquid siftings of the moon,
eating the baby's tongue, she whirls naked
round and round the live ant-hill.
I know old Tijah now goes covered with a shawl.

Within the abacus of my thought I cannot add
to the moon precise on the gashed up furrows.
Along stone corridors of the ordered hill
the wind crept unseen, divorced of leaf-voices.

No ghosts inhabit those dark trees by the hill-side,
only the passing of a habitual rain,
mist, white at evening out of the damp
dying and harsh longing of thrusting boughs:
nothing, but is fugitive, as when the heart is upon false scent
the dogs keep up their howling for the hour
before an early moon is down.

There is no commerce with the ghosts of those who died.
Out of the coming and passing of the words
my tongue finds for longing, from tangle of this dying,
there is but a little falling of damp earth
and a slight cold wind against the trees,
savagely intent upon their separate interior lives.

Keeping its days and seasons,
the land yields no speech to us
even through intercession of imagined ghosts
who would make it easier for the tongue.
Against the rain, nothing of the memory of the dead
is caught and held on among the roots.
The *merbak* in the shift of weather in a passing cloud,
makes for the mute stones and trees their words.

I feel out of the verges of the swamps
in the body's tides, out of the bones
of an ancient misery,
the dead stir with this advent of rain;
and in a landscape too long
in the contours of a personal anguish,
assume its presences: hedges and barb-wire,
trees in the numbness of the field;
and, moving in the dark between the houses,
conjure the heart
to breed upon the hint of a primal terror.
In the settling cold, I reach
beyond distances of a train's cry
beyond the mind's immediate neighbourhood
where the wind makes much of a tree in pain.

The legend the dead bear in the shifting rain
extends the habitations of a private landscape
which in the light of morning
upon a fallen hill-side and mud about
the hedges in a suburb that few think upon
will bring no change of heart
or hint for our new roof-lines.
Word of the terrible dragon's descent
upon a neighbouring hill will pass
in the breaking prism of the rain,

leaving houses and suburban roads in the cold and wet
and nothing to plague the dreams of children.
In its passing, I stare upon the quiet,
the mild hysteria of *lallang*, green under road-lamps.

There is no rumour as you would hear
coming too late
in neither time nor place for terror
but the quiet streets
and clocks keeping their hours
above the repetitive street-lamps in a town asleep.
No rumour as you would hear,
only that the lorongs turn
from the emptiness to twist about their dark,
articulate sometimes with violence
which has only brute recognition of the body's blood,

nothing of the imagined echo
that people were open to
when stones were known to prate.
There can be no rumour that terror is in the trees
or in the water below the bridge you cross
in the early light of morning,
having come in a time and place
too late to happen on claw-marks upon the pavements
or hear of a legendary half-beast
on certain nights clamber out of the municipal fountain.

This is only a body I possess
a body that bears a heart

weighted by its necessity, lost
in such a time and place
among a people who, when they came,
already had their demons
die the sterile deaths of gods:
so too their legendary kings.
This branch of cut lime
hung by my amah by the door
dangles therefore lightly in the breeze.

Yet do not believe
we do not have our kings,
do not believe
we take them lightly either.
We have our ways of submission
although, one having died,
our water does not turn bitter,
only the clerks glad of one day off.
The wind does not whimper.
You will not come suddenly upon him
around a corner, looming large
in the haze of a lamp.
Only, we have our ways of submission.

A few remember when we were small
how the dragon came,
and the floods
three months after the funeral of the King.

viii

Even the film-makers will have to admit,
the Malay annals upon the people's consciousness
would wash like the tide
piling flotsam against the jetty steps,
you said, as the car hit
ninety, beetling into our obsessive shell
of a parched landscape. And K.L. hours behind.
Dodging the disappearances and appearances
of the road, the cradled ego growing blind
against the body's chafing, would hide
from the terrible squashing of the sun,
threshing on daydream played out in the streets...
Of the Capitan China, the one
who, obscured in private vision,
laid down his law and had his women,
drove through the town in his carriage and eight -
for our forefathers left much behind
bringing mostly, when they came, the body
to contend with, did not notice the landscape,
the nodding vacuity of a malformed head.

At year's end, a sense of annunciation touched only
the windows of the solitary.
And at the garden-party, the bishop,

between meeting the community leaders,
picked at his beard, thinking perhaps of his study,
colonnades... the old cathedral town...
The Capitan's horses go clip-clop
passing like the breeze down the midnight streets.

Our conversation petering out...silences.
Day-dreams settle into laterite and gibberish of vegetation
which made nonsense of Saint Francis' mission.
De Sequeira's troops over the ridge
forgot the meaning of their Christ and King.
Under the flare of the sun's declension,
the hills ignited. We passed the region
of the dead, the circular descent of those
who died and had committed nothing.

Our room's on the second floor.
I am rather tired after to-day,
I feel the darkness of Babylon at the door.

Broken off from their daily pre-occupations
the streets on Sunday settle into their presences of stone.
Houses under a manic sun put up their distressed faces
and trees along the edges of a public lot
die quietly and to themselves. The walls remain
to keep the minotaur to the dark backstreets
when the heart, too much in the sun of its inconsequence,
is withered of its images: from its dark recesses
of jungle pool, the promised emanation of a god,
and rumour wild among the people, who would be saved
in the ruin of merchants and a lean year upon the fields.
But that images should wither and die,
weathered from the places where we would walk,
the buildings carry symptoms of our particular hell.
About the empty market square
we do not gather like agitated elders
in expectation of a runner in with the news,
the invaders held by the few at a narrow mountain pass,
bearers of good news being no more of the fashion.
You who would look for signs, or starve
among a wilderness of stone, there are only the boulders
drowning in pits of worked out mining leases.
From the main street of the town,
see how the hills are distant, locked in their silences.

Too long about this neighbourhood has palled
the mind to reaches of the suburban rail-track
bearing trains to nearby and expected places.
Feelings assume the twists and tangles of vegetation,
blukar clutching the soil from the weather
working upon the face its subconscious changes.
Coming to these suburbs by night, the heart
was crowded as all the public houses in the town,
the streets uneasy at the coming of a strange birth.
Once terror was real as the running about the streets,
the pain of looking for answers,
or resisting the king's soldiery at the door.
Too much in this weather has dissipated
the torment of the flesh's complexities,
as after the event, one becomes merely fretful
and eyes the neighbour's wife. On a clear night
the houses show up homely behind their hedges.
Driving upon the roads that lead from one to another,
there is with me the strange beast,
indifferent to the stars that ignite
heart's phosphorus, disintegrating towards the west.

I watched the dawn flowering out of a long wound
in the sky's side, across the anguish of roof-tops
the few trees disclosed, branches and their leaves
metal against my heart still raw with dream.
Out of my window I watched the scatters of swallows
spiral, tugging against tentacles in the streaks of cloud
and I too was unwilling for the dawn - when I must feel
discovered like the city: its fastnesses, drains
open, delineated like veins. In the blood
of the people's sleep the beast turned over upon its side
and moaned.

  As the hour struggled towards fruition in the sun,
buildings grew tall with my oppression, and I thought
of the many recalled, the broken and poor in spirit
scoured from their paleolithic womb of darkness.
I knew there was weeping, secret by the cataracts of the heart,
but that has nothing of the sadness of rivers or small rain,
mist making lyric all the low trees in the field,
the heart admitting only a purgatory paved of our familiar streets,
columns and walls of buildings lit, harsh in the devouring sun.

Where the blind fringes of my words
let in the symptoms of a dawn
breaking its anguish
over the hard indifferent pavements,
and loneliness in the bone engenders
this grotesquerie of faces under streetlamps,
women who pace their incarceration in empty streets,
I may be ready for the torment which infects
a new beginning - to be my lute's flame
to charm these manic buildings, the columns
and mindless walls, withholding monsters,
kindling the lost ease of swaying boughs
and swifts under a mild sun, to sue
out of a paranoiac darkness for a forgotten eurydice.

Rimbaud:

From the first, when the fire would no longer catch,
you, out of the doused flames,
the dried blood smoking in your face,
from the damp logs, the pyre of your vision,
would emerge, not the magi invoking
new flowers, new stars, new flesh and languages,
but the fierce, the charred mute
upon whom the flesh would always close again
to feel the inevitable first shock
of the rain's invasion, the abstract hunger
of pavements outside the tall cathedral door,
and hear the express ravening in from the suburbs,
from sunsets behind chimneys where your cloudy tragedians,
losing assurance, become the black beast to prowl in your sleep.

You who have prospected a little and gone
a little of the way, beyond the back-fences
of homes without a history, the rail-track and old estate
with its shallow streams, and found certain indications:
a change of colour in the soil,
the sudden scream of passing bird making huge
your anxiety upon the hill-slopes and then
a heart given to less frequent changes to clement weather,
beware - beware that you do not chance upon the hunger
that has taken prey of the time, come upon the hidden places
where loneliness uncoils within your bowels
and rises magnified, sheer in the granite hill-face:
the death the cobra bears for the lonely, who know no solution,
take care that such death does not work within your bones.

the inquisitors:

When they shall come again,
I do not know
where I shall hide in this consciousness
that makes distant, in this vast
plain of the damp floor
under the cell's black and foetid sky,
the congealed lotuses of my pain
dangling from the nails of my fingers
and in my bowels, the stiff bright sword.

When they shall come again,
I will feel anew the uselessness
of weeping. In the crumbling of houses
in the first destruction,
I knew there were children too among the ruins.
Yet there are times
the wind sings sweetly in the head,
and I whimper among the boughs
of dark unreason when
it wakens upon the ripples of mining pools.

I will be beaten down to their will,
my thoroughfares despoiled by instruments;
out of the ruins and re-opened tombs

I will not see you come, and go out upon the streets,
to tell the lame to walk and the blind to see.
You will not be there
when I shall be hunted out among my childhood -
only the relief of darkness
from the body's distant habitations
across the vast plain of the floor
and the cell's foetid sky.

To most only the despair is real,
winding from the face by rough steps
upward to the overwhelming hill
of Calvary, and the long deep strikes of pain
into the shoulder, as the dragged heavy end
of the cross, knocks in the teeth
of the lower steps following the ascent.
The mean fact of houses bars the way
crowding upon the lonely self,
and bare walls that hide our weeping in the garden.
There is only the self in the midst of fire -
when the planted crown strikes root
upon the skull
the agony beats back the overhanging Roman sun
and the multitude pressing in upon the hour
told in the sky's final desolation.
To most who after, turn away,
there cannot be wine-rows upon the slopes,
but the wind sawing at ruined walls
and a hint of bones in its tracks across the sands.

Words for an epiphany - for Wignesan

"I am the pitiful christ, nailed
to my birth
here, where they have no use for causes
or the agony I become,
redeeming nothing,
                              waking
to this brutal residue of stone
after the epiphany
of the body's pain, the dog
dragging its broken hind-legs
from the road,
                              the lost christ
among the fumes of the town's backstreets.

Let the locomotive jump its rails
and houses fall...

I will make dices of their finger-joints,
these legionnaires
gaming for shirt and sandal.
I strangled my mother-in-law
bearing the futility of it all,
this anguish of useless conversations

at coffee tables, hotel beds,
the opening darkness of the town's backstreets.

Let the locomotive jump its rails
and houses fall..."

xviii

For a birthday

To be most myself is to be
this darkness that pervades the land,
to be, in this foul weather, a climbing up
the turning wooden backstairs
to a rainless sleep, and in the morning,
in the small hours of the soul,
the cold that comes, making large
the doorways - the body in its spell
is a scatter of small stones beneath the porch.

This then is a country where one cannot wish
to be. The spirit not given its features
festers in the flesh, incites the year
to come upon it like the tiger. The city's parks,
odd street corners and the public buildings
bear the stench, the torn fur
of trivial remembrances. Thus in the flesh
am I hunted out, creature of my days,
vocal perhaps to seem some kind of Job

tending my sores to an emptiness,
the hoarse throat my psaltery to make such sounds
as may breed some hint for the soul's endurance.

Who would be comforters, do not begin to dress
or even touch these scabs -
their peeling leaves
a spreading terrain
where all conclusions, all arguments are broken down
to miles of striations, the soft mud-flats.

Batu Lane, K.L. - for Wignesan

When Navar became sixty, he was retired
from the life he had never been, from the boardroom,
airport receptions, from the Club 3 he had never been;
always anxious
before the steps of tall buildings,
finding himself from his wife, who for him has never been real,
or in the light of coffee stalls, beating
against the drunken darkness.
                                         It may well be...
The saints have testified, a going back upon the soul
is a going inward into the dark. The shoeshine
who lays out his tins, brushes and dirty rags
by the road, merely pushes from his dark
to lay his stakes against the tide,
the trafficking of humanity.
                                   For seven nights now
I have not touched my books, the distance
of neighbours moving in their rooms
has become estranging, making my exile the moonrise
over the lake of Li Po's words. To-night
the hibiscus bloom under the window
in the slats of light for a faceless hunger
in my ceils. Sickness has made real
the fever in the crooked trees, the moonlight
coming strangled into the garden,

and in the marshes of my bed, the snake's
distensions of the washes of my lust.

                                The backlane

I have sought out tunnels into its dark, narrowing into the intent
of each that enters, opening inwards
under the hanging moods of its towering
raintree, and on the one side the walls
of shophouses faintly white
with the faces of those garbled in their meaning.

Within, the dark is narrowed upon its heat and damp.
The main road across the range of roofs
is charmed away into the distance, into the past
of some non-arriving future, till one becomes
its moment to moment, the foul drains,
trishaws by the struggling hedges and garbage mounds
in the light of broken lamps
lighting these confines of sickness.
And then the lane opens onto a settlement.
Till then I could not have guessed, how
I am the many who wander in the mazes
infected with the ruin, the breaking
and the insides falling away without pain,
much as decaying houses with foetid rooms
crowding together upon the passages
that open at intervals onto cement courts. So many
the women here - grown indifferent to their flesh
it is useless to feel for so many -
sitting on low stools, or on their haunches by their doors,

silent, or hurt behind loud conversations.
When in a slant of light you catch the eye of one,
behind the stiffening of the face
you see the crouched, helpless, the stunted unfinished creature
that resides in your flesh, a moment, and is gone -
behind preparations against the assault upon her person,
raised under the red-eyed hostile stare.

There is upon the beacheads of my sleep,
the beating of the tide to toll the dead,
the drowned, thrown up upon the wreckage of daily living.
The night clambers in through
the open windows to root among the flesh's defeat.
For the stranded, among the stench of sea-weed
and the crabs, there are no gods
to propitiate. Ulysses scattering
the sacrificial blood of the white ram
upon the sand, plays merely the fool -
in the wind's talk - at most the gladiator
dressed to take the zebra crossing
in the busiest part of town. There are no shrines
Inland the terrain is locked in salt
where the beasts and the fowls of the air
lay down their bones by bitter lakes.
There are no pilgrimages but into the rocks' madness
at noon or their whimpering in the chill by night.
Let the shadows upon the rocks
number among losses. This is a time to endure
camping upon the lonely beaches,
content not to take much stock
by shooting stars, auguring the advent of sails.

Nocturnes and Bagatelles

i

Our Quarrel

Because I acted callously,
I left you
widowed upon your doorstep
with your dower of tears
withheld from the indifferent high door
and the suddenly important
wire-netting round the flowering lime.
I left you cradling your hurt,
the snapped ends of old twigs showing blood,
under the dull reality of an electric bulb
lighting the porch. The light pressed in
upon your person, already given
to the pawing of half-men. vestigial in the windy trees.

Because I acted callously,
I woke in the night thinking of you
to the infinite
loneliness of the empty curtains
the yellow room-light picking out
the heap of my soiled clothes
you had piled in the corner.
I heard above the distant stray bark of some dog,

an infant crying behind windows,
discovering the incipient tubers of my pain.
The flesh will yield to their pushing
when the image of your hurt becomes the ghost
bright in the inhospitable terrain growing out of your absence.

ii

The landscape lies taken under a hard sky,
under a wind dripping with rain
torn against frigid branches of the trees.
In my garden, the *frangipani* whiten like stones.

Evening settles in under a flat sky
upon a heart stricken with its emptiness.
You will not look upon my house, my broken garden
with *frangipani* by wire-fence strung with rain.

iii

The river grows harsh at the bend,
speech broken onto boulders, tears at root ends
of strong reeds. A lizard moves
and crawls in the mimosa
which spread and trail leafless
across the rough stones of my heart.
This is not the season
when the wind blows wet
and in the night rumours of the water fowl
but of the lonely sun
when anger withers on the stony bank,
its branches bare
against the sky that holds your absence.

iv

How long must I bend
in this uncertainty
I in my thought like flowers
toward every uncertain light,
how long must I labour
working from every bud
which folds within its calyx my emptiness
toward each spoor of rain
that I in my separateness
should move toward
full flowering of the human
that my words may quicken
with the grief and laughter
of every alien heart.

v

In your coming to my heart, my house,
choosing my dower, garnered
from hubandry of sweet usages of the self,
let trees that peal my love in flowers
peal their broad carillons
and egrets transfigured stand witness in rain,
while the landscape wounded to the stone
comes round with its many voices again.

vi

What movement of the mind
can release laughter,
uncover no dyke
against the coming in of time,

what mirage behind that face
now set in ebony
transfigured gradual ruin
working on that lyric Egyptian grace?

vii

Rummaging among my thoughts I went down their steps
to the cellar with a bundle of words
as matches to throw up areas of light upon the clammy walls
and I left my shadow at the door, substanceless, unheard.

Here were the tangles of my childhood - half-dreams
propelled, lifting the trap-door off my heart,
me on the violence of the garden swing -
twitching like half-torn snakes, buried in part.

It seemed, from the light where bushes felt really green
with the familiar air of a well-off merchant,
I have been summoned by unformed voices I left behind
to come to the cellar to set my house in order

to rationalise in neat parcels, the sky
that turned like a bald face over the circular garden-walk
over the child on the swing who gave his orang-outang
identity, its irrational leer behind bougainvillae stalks.

viii

For my old amah

To most your dying seems distant,
outside the palings of our concern.
Only to you the fact was real
when the flame caught among the final brambles
of your pain. And lying there
in this cubicle, on your trestle
over the old newspapers and spittoon,
your face bears the waste of terror
at the crumbling of your body's walls.
The moth fluttering against the electric bulb,
and on the wall your old photographs,
do not know your going. I do not know
when it has wrenched open the old wounds.
When branches snapped in the dark
you would have had a god among the trees
make us a journey of your going.
Your palm crushed the child's tears from my face.
Now this room will become your going, brutal
in the discarded combs, the biscuit tins
and neat piles of your dresses.

ix

I must make self-murder that I live,
cauterise love at the root of sense
till deceit and all that pain
wither with body's recalcitrance.
　　　　But words alone do not resurrect
　　　　dog what wets the bottom of those steps.

I must make self-murder that I live,
and batter the ego in his bed
till deceit and all that pain
be out with heart on which it bred.
　　　　But words alone do not resurrect
　　　　dog that wets the bottom of those steps.

　That soul should elbow its way
　and not stay clear
　leaving, for all its neighbourliness
　the body harder to bear,
　that of body I should sour
　its giving of itself
　rape sense and throw it out-of-doors
　making it more stubborn by half,
　transmute of this brawl the shards
　into formal pain of words.
And words alone will not resurrect
dog that wets the bottom of those steps.

There is a germinal use in violence -
the felling of trees in the jungle, and after,
spilling of the kampong's recalcitrance
in its desperate ultimate slaughtér.

The dead, in their ceremonious brocade,
littered where, sailing up-river, the aliens
had broken the stillness with their ambuscade.
They brought new perspectives to our human situation.

Wild pigs snorted among the dead at night,
Perhaps the monkeys too, were appalled at this,
time's seeming necessary rite
for its giving birth to other promise.

That he cared a little less for his habitual image
of himself, the bamboo hedges and the tall palms
leaped with the sudden flame of morning.
That he should acknowledge pain of unfinished lineaments
the cannas unfurled, yellow and huge in unaccustomed freedom
and the play of sparrows among thick leaves would serve for words.
The distance unwound itself of muscular clouds,
unwound his guard over his secret places of inadequacies.
The hills with hidden water-courses and valleys bearing rain
came close to his touch. From the fire the gardener lit in wet piles of grass.
the smoke hung all day beneath the trees.

When you walk in the *dusun*,
the flying foxes gone,
mangosteens tightened up in knots
on shrivelled boughs, be glad
the heart too can turn up root
and die.
                    Done with laying
of ghosts and things seen
by the dogs barking all night
when scent of the turned earth
is upon the wind.

At the house the rafters sag.
Fear deserts by way
of the high stilts with the mice.

The heart then makes with dying:
leaves drying, litter
the sour ground.
In the old *dusun*
the boughs throw shadows
that fall sharp upon the earth.
There is no sound
of love-making animals or birds.

When the heart is stripped and bare
there is only the earth,
old roots,
wind that has no hunger
and calm expanse of sky.

II

For a Local Osiris

Candles For a Local Osiris

(For the maimed and the dead, as partisans)

Encourage your heart to forget it, making it pleasant
for your to follow your desire whilst you live.
                              - Song of the Harp Player

i

The sea pulls back from its mangrove edges,
from the houses subverted into mud.
Upon tendons of the wind's throat, vestigial,
and rasping against the bared roots feeding on
the mud rows, the drowned play out their dream -
phosphorescences, creatures and driftwood.
And here, growing urgent upon the smell
of the soul's disaster, I confront your death.
The flares strung out to the jetty's end
burn for your death, burn for a sick consciousness,
the wharves where debris of old crates and wagons
smoulder with its hurt, for the great ship
crawling out across the water, towards the islands,
towards the sky, as you leave these tides to beat upon
estuaries new to this gathering dark.

To be forced back by the undertow
that swells in the tide among the channels
and a rising wind, to be washed adrift
upon the mystery of your going, beyond those islands,
is to come back not wholly intact - to return,
the body awkward with its old certainties,
conscious of a sickness to which all are open
who suffer the first wounds breaking
of the solitary.

Overtaken in the closing darkness
that comes after uncertain hint of knowledge,
I am oppressed by dream
of the many savaged within their sleep.
Murdered into a kind of waking, they make
no lament of dismemberment.

iii

Whenever the night is troubled with the wraiths
of rain that haunt our roofs, stirring the senses
and, in the blood, a carnivorous waking
only to the reek of the city's promises,
I think of your death. A god, that day you stalked
your quarry till a sudden clearing in the woods
happened on you and its changes of climate
coursed through your veins. The flowers
you found here were furry and green
and could not bloom. In the undergrowth, the thing
you surprised had the look you did not understand.
And when remembrance of what you had done,
or left undone, could no longer hurt you
like a wound, under the leafy shadows
you were made ready for death.

iv

Out by the back way past closing time
I make for the road. Through worn soles the loose stones
hurt. My toes feel moist from pressing into slush.
Raw trash on a chill wind... Out there my disquiet
spreads, infests the mounds piled high, fermenting
in the wide-mouthed municipal bins. Whatever moves,
moves among greased cans, bruised tomatoes and things
spilt form plastic bags...

Only once have I sensed it,
high above the roadway, above the sodium lamps that light
the nearby intersection, hard against the sky, adrift -
drawn from the sea by rankness of these breeding grounds.
With savage beak and claw, you would have wrought
much havoc, cast terror wide before you
as you slipped into the plunging bright arc of your descent.

This city which whitens before mid-morning
into the furnace of the overhanging sun
is place of your absence. All is adrift:
mazes of short streets; sudden intersections
where the traffic, stalled, is laid out in miles
of fuming junk; lopped trees; steam-hammers blasting in
more certainties for the spreading landscape
of towers, bridges, car parks, overpasses... Dust
swirls in the clear, hard fire of the small noon sun.
Your absence leaves this city to the governance
of men who know no surprises in their waking dream -
or touch of sun. So in the happy hour, the rush
begins of massed vehicles pressing for the outer darkness
or westward to suburbs among low hills
set hard against the soft, red, gigantic ball of fire.

vi

Song

I hesitate at the gate, the moonlight
tindery, as the garden of my certainties
would crumble at a touch
and the land return to silence huge as thunder.
I hesitate at the gate, bearing your death,
the season's wound, as nightjars
lodged in the trees make
peculiar comfort of their round burden of dumbness;
afraid to enter, though the flesh
is loud elsewhere with its dying,
as I would not meet in my narrow bed,
the savagery of the heart
howling in a dream of quiet towns,
of fallen bridges where the water
passes in coils of its own dark will.

Shrine by the rail track

The tiles fallen about you, the whitewash
peeling about the cheeks, the eyes set
and blind with meaning, thinking on your face,
O Lady, make more real the glitter of disaster
about the brittle grass and upon the trees
which shadow the pathway to the shrine
from the rail track, its white stones explosive
under the sun...

        Remembrance
has a hint within your blindness
of the soul's horrible journey
into its metamorphoses.
Held in granite is a kind of waking,
the stir of a god's limbs
across a field of rising waters...
and in the soft earth, glistening, the insects...

viii

The first signs would almost go unnoticed
like the bruised flowers, the crushed stalks
in the chrysanthemum beds discovered mornings
under the window. In hours of the lightest sleep
there had been something opened the garden gate.
Your coming has always been an unease in the bone.
When the time breaks, the house dog will whine
and whimper upon the hour. There would be those
would sense you behind the woodshed, among the stand of trees in the
falling light, waiting. Nothing would help
stanch the gathering smell of our mortality.
Always you have been everywhere about us.
When the time breaks, we are still to come to terms
with loneliness, look out without terror on the darkness thick
behind you, as you make your way in by the gate.

Envoi

Though there be little comfort, you will tear your hair
and groan upon the ground after you lose your nerve
and things you call up turn into monsters
clawing at the folds of your clothes, their snouts
crazed at the scent of your dying, begun in the mind.
The light upon a common landscape hurts your eyes
when the caul is ripped with which you would cover
your mortality. There is something escapes you
about the stranger whose face is leprous under the road lamp
and his face clogged with new earth,
or else you may still make the trees to lean to you
and still the murderous smoking yellow behind the eyes
of gigantic cats. Too long about the same spell,
wearing it thin, leaves you an evil-smelling,
unwashed prophet railing at bus-stands at indifferent crowds.

Osiris Transmogrified

Men's fears are buried deeply by repression, which
gives to everyday life its tranquil facade...
> - Ernest Becker, ESCAPE FROM EVIL

i

You startled me, leaning over the headstone,
leaning out of my anxieties which broke
to cloud the air, the high wind from which the swifts
in showers of black stones plunged then rode with wings
distended the undertow that racked up waves
of *lallang* flowing up the cemetery hill.
Your disappearance left me in a dull
and orange light, seeing the first time in
my hand the bunch of rust red chrysanthemums
to mark the place, the mound, depository of bones
cleansed of all flesh, all trace and scent that had been
Father, left me as some other standing on dried mud
tracked around the terrazzo-topped, limestone
and concrete table, his oblatory slab.

You came up on me again in the streets,
whispering of a dreadful awakening,
of consciousness dislodged, wrenched loose from thick
sea-bed, to eye in a troubled stream, in altered light,
the crowd, each face, each along the five-foot ways
caught up in a dense current of his own cold
and ichthyic dream - of scent of blood
in dim water, of small life to be dredged up
and filtered through teeth into lipless mouth.
The watcher holding itself still among the reeds
was thinned out into nothingness, into banks
of water, opaque as smoked glass, blue-green,
impervious. Out of such deep glass clouding into slate,
no brutal engulfing darkness would break through.

This house, these walls that gave back to the room
the warm lamplight, identity and place
could not keep you out. You came through as shadow
as if the night. the sky's, the earth's black
had resolved itself into a mist to flow through,
break out in faint grey from beneath the new whitewash.
In the cold hours, a wind of desolation rose
out of the heart's wastes and swept through all
the unlit rooms, the doorways. In my sleep you turned:
in the single flame of a candle, a presence,
you made a habitation of the moist twilight
about the shrine, the weeds, the rubble
falling out from under collapsed timber in the air-well
of an abandoned construction site.

                      You were a shadow
assuming form - a beast, elemental god
incarnating, sprawled upon damp sacks, old newspapers,
trousers opened at the fly. The limbs and torso
in their bulk were not fully resolved from mud.
Thinking to look closer, I drew you out and saw -
the face, an earth wall, cutting that had slipped
under the weight of rain and, in that featureless wound,
myself, sheared of all familiarity grown from long
having been human. In the morning, I was smooth
hard stone rolled over the sea-bed in a rising
stream. The children going up and down the stairway
were carried luminescent in half-light - yellows,
greens and blues and pinks - roundels turning
in the stream - afloat, migratory, bright sea-anemones.

Address from the God

Where the vegetation swells with such force
as erupts from the gound, bursts into day
in great streams, geysers,green rolling waves,
there have I returned. A boiling tide,
I have covered this city over, this earth,
racked it in your own passions - to procreate,
prey, eat others of your kind - and driven deep
through the narrows, the hard round channels of my roots
into your buildings, walls, your secret recesses,
through pavements into laterite to push and edge,
dislodge the sides of hidden wells, in black earth
let break violent waters as would move your dreams
and force into subsidence great beds of stone
along deep faults beneath your breathing city.
It is for you to find your way about
the cataracts, up-swelling wash and torrents
in this pouring out, immanence of your god,
fattening jungle greening to the point
of madness. If, in your head, the moon is right,
you might catch in the undertow, thick surge of growth
here, there, about the base of trunks, through vine
and fern, images of a life which shows
its flanks, face half-hidden or paws emerging
out of a past, an imagined future. Your way
from here would close in to the jungle's own
still sub-aqueous chambers where others who

into the black and green have gone before
now feed a ground-swell that has its force begin
where time is not, or place. Where a low branch swings,
green fingers rise and spread out in the tepid stream;
live bark over disturbed, wounded trunks of trees
swells into rough mounds, would close over captured
somnolent faces... There is no shrine here,
no benign god - but devourer who moves
in the life of vegetation broken out of their bounds
of darkness, who would take you whole and spew
you out only as a pair of beating lungs,
as heart, liver and genitals and as maw
ravenous in the jungle's floor for dead
meat and flies and such forms of life
not warmed by blood. Even if the light should shift
and the whole green flood should rise and disappear
thinly and the wind blows free across the city's
clear and sunlit face, in the shadows you will still
be racked by brown-scaled dragons carrying their scent
among the drains, the rubbish bins, breeding places
of mice, of mud-fish, white worms, insects that cover
in thick clouds the orange flares that line uneasy streets,
some leading out of dense black gaps in sleep.

III

What Are the Roots...

Readings from Tu Fu - A.D.712-770
(For Lloyd Fernando)

i

Prospect in spring

At the death of great houses,
the waste of cities,
the land returns to desolation
of its rivers and its hills.
The high walls under a mild sun
lie fissured, opened in great wounds
to the ravening tide of spring.
These flowers that well up from the ground
are tears I weep
against adversity.
I think of you my children. My fear
darkens around this chirruping
of sparrows fighting beneath the walls.
The skies these nights are louring, red
with beacon fires built for the invasion.
I would there were news from home.
Daily the comb slips more easily through my hair.
Of little use my passions...
This hairpin in my fingers,
it will not catch, then falls
from the hair onto the palm.

Late revels

A slender moon is setting among tree-tops
of the prowling wind. We sit, ambushed
in the lute's dark melody,
our clothes long wet with the risen dew.
The flowers grow tall
in the ministering dark, and among the skeins of grass,
the stars. The night burns, too short
like a scholar's candle,
for our ensuing talk of swords and embroidery among wine-cups.
Our verse recited
moves with the lightness of a skiff,
passing into waters where the sky recedes
into the horizons of another speech,
another place, another time.

iii

Spring night in the imperial chancellery
(On the eve of a court levee)

These walls, ablaze all day with a show
of flowers, now begin fading into dusk.
In its deepening gulfs, thin cries of late birds
tell of their pushing into darkness still.
Stars thicken. Brightening into fierce grains of fire
over the open doorways, they come close to the touch.
The moon, still low-hanging, a breaking orange flame,
will soon whiten into a bursting radiance in mid-sky.
In the hollow silence of these halls
I start at the imagined turning of the high bronze doors,
at bridle-bells, drifting in brittly on the wind.
There is the Sealed Memorial for the morrow.
Shut out from sleep, I ask constantly about the hour
but fail to hasten passage of the night.

River journey by night

Wind moves in the disturbed thin grass on the bank
and about the boat as its solitary tall mast
cuts a way over uncertain waters into night.
Over the void stars splinter, scattering fine grain -
at the sky's edge, at the empty plain's. The moon
comes up at me from the water, an incandescent,
live thing screaming to break free
from the turning black coils of the moving flood.
Drifting my way into these wilderness, I find
an end to having to make something of my name,
an end to the counting of losses...and image
of a self - grey gull tossed upon fierce winds,
falling forever into the sky, finding no earth
to come back to, even momentarily, for foothold.

Moonlit night

To-night, a full moon,
and you alone again.
I think often of the children,
too young to feel my absence here in Ch'ang-an.
Your hair must be laved with dew
and your limbs cold.
I do not know when I can return...
to be with you behind the empty curtains,
the tear-stains on our faces bright in the moon.

vi

In the north

This is an autumn of clear chill fires...
At the well's edge trees, iron and black, stand
surprised by the cold. The light chastens...
Alone in my quarters I feel, to-night,
my spirit gutter, my single candle fail
in the stench of its molten heap of wax.
Out of unending night, around the fort,
come the bleak self-communings of bugles.
The moon now in full ascendance makes
of the heavens a radiant field of light,
makes little of the chaos lodged within.
Where convulsions of the times have gouged
from the land farms, markets, fields and cities,
there can be no more hope of word from home.
I am adrift, cut off in these northern wastes
beyond desolate passes, beyond bad roads.
I count this but one night of unmolested
wakefulness, holding down dreams - bird
blown in from battering winds to roost among
bare boughs dying at the coming of the ice.

Thinking of my brothers in time of war

All roads are now overtaken by great tumult of drums
rolling their thunder at the sky from fields of war.
At the frontier, autumn turns upon the call
of a solitary wild goose in the chill, grey wastes.
The moon, these nights, drifts like a ghost
through wide swathes of mist over plains of whited dew...
It blooms in the memory, bright over harvest fields.
Where once home was, weeds invade the doorways
and snakes the filled-in wells.
All my brothers... all were fired like foxes from the lair.
Who now is still alive? Who dead?
Of whom shall I enquire? But no word will come,
not till a trampling soldiery is drawn from the field
and rested from the carnage they bring upon the land.

From a height

Here all is blinding sky, and wind spewing out
of the void in great turning spouts and tides.
Streams dredge up with the ice, wild, sad cries
of gibbons miles below. Islands, sandspits,
white flecks of circling cranes are cleansed by distance -
even the woods, dying in their slow autumnal fury
which wreaks a bald ruin across the land.
Inexhaustible as time, the river pours
its life out in fierce, bright gouts of water -
while my life itself has wound its way into a field,
a waste of dead trees, churned up mud and ice.
Into its silences I have now lost my way.
Deep depression makes me sicken at the fumes -
from bad wine strained from dregs - that cloud my cups,
bloom into mild haze in the worst of weathers.
With spirit and bone still badly healing
I have come - push this body to make the ascent.

Taoist Poems
(After Li Po - A.D.701-761)

i

Waiting for a friend at his retreat

Cutting through the waters that swell
the hanging cataracts among these hills,
a dog's disembodied barking drifts
with the thunder across thick pines
upon a lifting wind. A stand of blossoming peach
darkens, breaks out into cascades of rich blood
from the settling damp. As out of a dream
red deer startle, slip back into the standing wood.

Day gathers into noon. The bell that tolls the hours
in these hills dissolves into a nothingness.
Wild bamboo here curve into the depths of sky,
and, in the distance, from clear strong springs,
bright spouts of water tear off from the face
of moss green peaks and fly into a rolling wind.
It is not given me yet to know the place,
find you in the deep recesses of these hills.

Caught up in thought, I lean against the rough bark
of one and then another of these tall pines.

Summer in the hills

This is a summer that smoulders in the flesh.
So, with all my clothes, I cast away my fan
and lie here naked, deep in these dense, green woods.
Up on that rock-face my girdle dangles in the sun.
The wind comes whistling from the mountain pines
and bathes my head in wide, cool and dreamless spaces.

iii

The heron

Heron drifting, settling out of the sky,
noiseless like frost over clear, autumnal waters
whitening the air from a sudden chill...
It folds into itself, into a single stone
white upon a barren spit; in its stillness, holds
the sky and, faintly in its depths, the receding sun.

Home thoughts

At my bed's feet my room ignites,
white with the moon's loneliness.
And I feel outside, the cold, incendiary
in the hard frost upon the ground.
I am full of the moon, on looking up,
hanging large above the window,
and in my dark, I meet, on looking down,
my fierce unsatisfied longing to be home.

Bidding farewell to a friend in a boat

We have drunk ourselves to numbness
becoming mere tissue, mere bone
upon whose damp even the lute's flame
has quenched itself. The night now
infects the light of our single lamp,
smoking it blue, and the moon,
as it turns chill once again, engenders
ice in the marrow. Our shouts, disembodied bits
of song and laughter drift with the mists,
like spirits wandering on the face of black waters.
The egrets are startled in their sleep.
The islands heave with a tumult of wings
as, in the small hours, the flocks rise,
abandon long spits of sand to the night.

At Lord Hsieh's in the country

Azure blazing under a white sun in these hills
will soon subside, blacken into its dying fires.
In failing light, desolation of the wilds
has crept into your fields, your house.
These drying stands of bamboo
straggle thinly outwards into the night.
The moon conceals itself like a strange white fish,
unmoving, noiseless in the pond,
breathing faintly from its depths.
Your outer court is now a field of weeds.
At the lips of old wells black moss gathers.
Where no light is, a mild wind stirs.
It flows all night like a river,
fed by small springs, turning over the smooth hard stones.

Into the hills

You wonder that I lose myself
into these blue hills.
My laughter closing upon silence
guards a quiescent heart.
Shed peach petals on the face of waters
flow with the living stream.
There is another earth, another sky
not of this world of men.

A mountain visit

The mountains here dissolve into the one blue
of the sky - into silence - towards a stillness
beyond the bounds of time. I grope my way up them
through descending banks of cloud, feel
for traces of an ancient trail. There is a bald tree
by which I rest and, all thought subsiding,
become the murmur, the cold, clear gush
and flow of an erupting mountain spring.
The flowers here bear warm imprint of having been
slept upon and in the sand, a clear hoof-print...
Cranes are chilled into white silence in tall pines,
some caught up in sleep among the branches in mid-sky.
I find the master in. Our conversation fades
with the light which turns rivers into slow veins
blackening on the far plains at the approach of night.
Alone, I stumble my way down into biting cold and fog.

Reading of a Tang Poem

About three years ago at a private party, one of those informal buffets where the guests are allowed to wander about the more "public" areas of the host's house, one of my fellow guests, a Chinese educationist, picked up from the host's bookshelves a copy of my "Remembering Grandma and Other Rumours". The poem that caught his interest was my version of Tu Fu's, "Prospect in Spring", which I had included in the volume. He said he liked the "translation", but being the eudcationist that he was, he could not resist grading it in accordance with his yardstick of fidelity to the dictionary meaning of the words of the original. It was re-assuring that he recognised the poem the moment he read it. It was not quite so re-assuring, that he awarded me only seventy marks for accuracy - not a good grade for a translation but a decent enough passing mark in an examination.

My interest in Tu Fu is a late, barely thriving germination of seeds which had lain dormant over the years since the days when I endured afternoon classes in Chinese language and literature. The staple of our curriculum was "Three Hundred Tang Poems", an anthology of three hundred poems compiled in 1764 of selections from forty-eight thousand nine hundred poems surviving from the Tang period (A.D.618-906) and the principal means of instruction consisted in the teacher directing us to memorise as homework one or two assigned poems and to write them out correctly to the last stroke and dot of each word the following day in class. Naturally the poems did not catch fire amongst us in class. The teacher's exegesis on the poems was quite lost on us as most of us were then still at the stage of our education when we dozed through Wordsworth and Masefield in morning school.

Years later, after I had taken an active interest in writing verse, bits of lines and imagery from the Tang poems began to surface in the memory. What I remembered of the poems looked very interesting. That prompted me to think about the possibility of putting the poems into English and saying, in the process, something about the Malaysian condition in ways I could not manage in my own verse. I have since worked in this way, with a few poems, without really reflecting on what it is that I have been attempting. If pushed to it, I will have to say that I have not been doing any translations. There has to be the necessary scholarship for this enterprise. Neither have I been attempting "imitations" in Robert Lowell's sense of the word in explaining his "imitations" of European poets. There is in imitations, with due respect to that great poet, an implication of plagiarism but he may be the one poet who is big enough to make this criticism seem not to matter. The alternative, "interpretations", sounds too much like an explanation of the one officially approved meaning of a text. For this, I do not have the authority. All I can claim for my versions is that they are personal readings of texts I like. In a reading, I can, at worst, be only wrong-headed and not actually wrong.

Differences in liguistic characteristics between classical Chinese and English are so great as to open up an almost unbridgeable gulf between the two languages. They make an academically "correct" and yet effective translation of a Chinese poem well nigh impossible. What is most frequently lost is the tone of the original. It is extremely difficult to carry that over from a language which is so terse that it can dispense with prepositions, subordinating conjunctions, subjects, for verbs, number, tenses and the passive voice into English, which insists on complete sentences in formal written texts. What sounds perfectly natural, serious, or grave even, in a classical Chinese text, can appear comic and sometimes platitudinous if, in bringing it over into English, the translator attempts to retain some authentic "flavour" of the original by imitating Chinese sentence structures and sound patterns, and by close individual matching of Chinese words with English equivalents. Yet it is these very difficulties that justify a greater freedom in translation than between more closely related languages. The terseness of the Chinese text may be exploited by the imagination to fill in "gaps" left unstated in it in more explicit English. This is the aesthetics which informs Chinese painting where a few bare brush strokes invite the viewer to enter into a landscape his imagination helps to create.

Because of the differences between the languages, I feel that the best strategy for rendering an English version of a Chinese text is to write it as if it is an original poem in English. This means putting out of mind altogether the linguistic characteristics of the original and giving what one understands to be the essential life of the poem recognisable form in the structures available in English. It was perhaps this freedom in the strategy I adopted that earned me the less than full approval of my educationist for the version of the Tu Fu poem given here as follows:

"Prospect in Spring"

At the death of great houses,
the waste of cities,
the land returns to desolation
of its rivers and its hills.
The high walls under a mild sun
lie fissured, opened in great wounds
to the ravening tide of spring.
These flowers that well up from the ground
are tears I weep
against adversity.
I think of you my children. My fears
darken around this chirruping
of sparrows fighting beneath the walls.
The skies these nights are louring, red
with beacon fires built for the invasion.
I would there were news from home.
Daily the comb runs

more easily through my hair.
Of little use, my passions...
This hairpin in my fingers,
it will not catch, then falls
from the hair onto the palm.

A consequence of writing the poem as if it is meant to be an original poem in English is an intensification of a subjectivity not found in the same degree in the Chinese text. This unavoidable falsification of the original comes from the presence of a strongly subjective organising "I" which, as subject of the poem's discourse cannot be left out as the grammatical subject in an English sentence. The only thing that can be said for it is that it is natural to the "grain" of the English language.

A translation which may be said to be closer to the spirit of a scholarly translation, such as my educationist may more approve of, is a recent one by Arthur Cooper (Penguin Books). Its first four lines read as follows:

> In fallen states
> hills and streams are found,
> Cities have spring,
> grass and leaves abound;
>
> Though at such times
> flowers might drop tears.
> Parting from mates,
> birds have hidden fears:
>
> - "Looking at the Springtime"

Each of the above stanzas corresponds to a couplet in the original, with each two consecutive lines forming a 4+7 syllabic pattern. This is in imitation of the 2+3 syllabic pattern of each single line of the original. In Chinese, the regular 2+3 pattern of syllables gives to the verse, in this instance, a serious and even tragic tone. It is a mystery of language that the same regularity of pattern, such as in Cooper's variation in the form of the 4+7 pattern, in English verse has the reverse effect of making it sound light, if not actually platitudinous. It trivialises the subject matter of the poem, I think. Cooper's first two lines in fact raises the question as to why only in fallen states are hills and streams found. Is "cities have spring..." meant to be a profound statement? Also, the sentence beginning with "Though" is logically not complete.

Mainland Chinese poet, Wu Juntao has the first four lines thus:

> As ever are hills and rills while the Kingdom crumbles,
> When springtime comes over the Capital the grass
> scrambles.
> Blossoms invite my tears as in wild times they bloom,
> The flitting birds stir my heart that I'm parted from home.

- "A Spring View"

Like Cooper, Wu attempts to stay close to the original in individual word meanings and verse pattern, as far English can be made to accommodate the latter. Though it says the same things as Cooper's version on the level of dictionary meanings and is made to parallel the regularity found in the Chinese text, it has the feel of a totally different poem, perhaps because Wu still thinks in Chinese. It shows that the essential life of the poem cannot be captured through importing linguistic devices appropriate to Chinese into alien English.

To make the matter clear, I quote the first four lines of the original with a transliteration of the sounds in Pin-yin:

國	破	山	河	在
gúo	pò	shān	hé	zài
state	broken	hill/s	river/s	exist/be at
城	春	草	木	深
chéng	chūn	cǎo	mù	shēn
city/city wall	spring	grass	wood	deep
感	時	花	濺	淚
gǎn	shí	hūa	jìan	lèi
feel	time/s	flower	spray	tears
恨	別	鳥	驚	心
hèn	bíe	niao	jīng	xīn
hate	apart	bird/s	frighten	heart

In my own reading of Line 1, I have not taken the English word equivalent for *"guo"* as "state". I have read the word in the sense of a feudal kingdom in times when the nation state was unknown. Therefore, the ruling dynastic family or the "great house" can reasonably serve as a surrogate for "state" which encompasses associations with "cities" since power was maintained by the ruling families out of heavily fortified cities. The fall of a state in those times meant also extermination of the ruling dynastic line and the sack of their cities. I have therefore not found it necessary also to read *"guo po"* narrowly as the "state falling" or "breaking" (which more accurately should be "breaking up" in English) of a state. The interesting word in Line 1 is *"zai"*, "to exist" or "to be present at". In juxtaposition with "hills" and "rivers" in the line, it has the connotation of something eternal, lasting from age to age as against dying generations of people. This, together with the wholesale putting to the fire and sword of settled communities implied by the destruction of the state, suggests the "desolation" of the land which reverts to the condition of unpopulated valleys and hills.

Line 2 is a parallel line to Line 1. The "deep woods and grass encroaching on the "city/broken battlements in spring" of the Chinese text suggests an overpowering nature, which easily reclaims the land from man's weak hold on it. (How different this sentiment is from to-day's environmentalist concerns). I have, in this reading, emphasized the active, voracious aspect of nature. The word *"shēn"*, "deep" in the context of the line suggesting thick, rank vegetative growth supports this emphasis. Lines 3 and 4 are also parallel lines. Cooper's and Wu's versions are two different but acceptable interpretations of the grammar of the lines. "Flowers" and "birds" are the only subjects of the sentences that make up the two lines in Cooper's version. In Wu's version, the sentence structure suggests the presence of an "I" who sees flowers and is moved to tears and who hears birds cry and becomes the more anxious for being parted from family (which could mean either wife or children or both). Wu's interpretation is the more usual in Chinese usage, while only Cooper's accords with correct English syntax. I have preferred Wu's interpretation in my reading. I have also fleshed out the scenarios only implied in the text.

Tu Fu wrote the poem at a time of upheaval in the Empire caused by the rebellion in 756 of the Tartar general, An Lu-shan. The Court had for years already been undermined by the corruption and incompetence of its officials and its hold on the administration of law and order weakened by endless taxes imposed on a disaffected populace to raise revenue to finance wars of expansion undertaken in the name of the Emperor and the extravagant spending of the palace on continuing festivities and useless building projects. The Emperor himself was dislodged from the capital at Chang-an and had the killing of his favourite concubine, Yang Kuei-fei, forced upon him by his officials at a way-station only forty kilometers out of the capital.

91

To-day the poem speaks to us still of the anxieties that come from the complete loss of a previously settled order. As inheritors ourselves of societies undermined by the advent of the West and, with it, the spread of an impersonal commercialism founded upon the exploitation of technologies and markets and ravaging of the environment for profit, we too must feel the moral ambiguities that reside at the heart of this loss. As much as Tu Fu himself, we hear of war and rumours of war as if war is a universal condition and, perhaps more than he ever felt, we are cut off from a "home" which is now forever beyond recovery. At the time when I "read" the poem, I was a great deal younger and could not quite manage the wry tone of the poet who sees himself as a sightly ridiculous balding old man, mortal and helpless in the face of great impersonal forces that swept through his time. More than ever we will need to have something of his capacity for not taking oneself too seriously in order to survive our own times.

A Version From T'ao Yuan-Ming
(A.D.376-427)

i

I had no taste, when young, for the world's affairs,
my heart native to the love of hills,
For thirteen years now I am fallen,
tangled in the deep snares of the world.

A caged bird is haunted by the old, dark woods,
in shallow ponds the fish, their former waters.
And so, I have returned
to farm upon the margins of the southern wild -

my land, a bare two acres
and my house, ruled into eight rooms or perhaps nine,
with the elm and willow leaning thick upon the eaves,
and in the court, the planted peach and plum.

The dwelling places of men are way in the distance
wreathed thinly with the smoke from market towns.
One hears only the barking of dogs among deep lanes,
the cocks crowing, hidden in the mulberry tops.

I am no longer visited with the world's desires,
my days made over with such large and ample ease.
My heart, long caged and corralled,
assumes now the major freedom of the hills.

In the wilderness where men's affairs are absent,
the narrow lanes empty of passing horse and carriage,
and houses remain shuttered in the sun,
I have put away my flesh's and the world's desires.

And at the times when the farmers gather
or meet by chance, going about in their grass capes
in the fields, they have but few words for each other.

Now is the season when the crops planted daily find increase
and the season when my purposes daily are fulfilled;
of anxiety at the coming frost and sleet
when as the tangled vegetation, I shall stand ruined and bare.

My bean rows grow sparsely under the southern hill,
strangled and choked by the coarse devouring weeds,
though I toil all day upon the wilderness, from daybreak
till darkness falling, when I grope my way home by the moon.
Till footpath is narrow with overhanging weeds.
My clothes are wet from the risen dew.
But then I should not care that my clothes are wet
when it is my purpose not to care.

It has been a long time since I went among the hilld and the marshlands, where in the solitude, the wild untrammelled weeds and trees pleased my heart, and I found my peace. I, an old man, must leave my children and those of my children's generation, and with a staff of hazelwood in hand, wander once more about the wilds.

Once in a desert place, I came upon a profusion of mounds and broken dykes about the habitation of a people of an earlier time. There are wells, choked and fallen in, and kitchens, broken open to the wind and rain. The straggles of bamboo and mulberry grew meanly over the untended ground.

When I asked of a passing wood-gatherer, he made in reply: All the people here have perished, man, woman and child, never to return.

A generation passes like a market fair. Truly, the living are but passing tricks and shadows, and a return to nothingness, our end.

I returned alone by the broken tortuous trails,
my heart full of the mountain's desolation.
At a torrent,
where the stream was bright and shallow, I washed my feet.
I strain the clear and new-made wine,
and with a capon serve my guests.
At the going down of the sun
we light brushwood to serve as candles.
Cloistered with a living joy of friends
how quickly the bitter dark will pass.
And then... a new daybreak.

IV

Rumours of Exits

A Death in the Ward

They had to change old Manickam three times
yesterday morning. Sunk among the dry sheets
he began to give up on the useless match-sticks
of his legs. His people brought him

only after they had found
they could do nothing much about his spells of retching.
All of his sixty-seven years were locked
inside his skull. Quite out of reach...

All day I dreamt fitfully, laid out in bed.
The fluorescent lamps from their high ceiling
hurt our eyes. We were clay-skinned, great deformed caterpillars
sealed in the quiet of this public ward.

The doctor told me I was down with jaundice.
All head and squashed body,
I dreamt I rose beating moth-like against the window panes.
Is this six o'clock in the evening?

When Manickam died in the night, they had no need to be gentle
with his body. By the reading light they stripped his bed.
It somehow crossed my mind
the contents of his stomach would be cold by the morning's autopsy.

In those small hours I saw I too had died.
How should the body discard itself? How should the flesh let go?
Down there, outside the darkened hospital grounds
they would be letting the truck in with the day's supplies.

And I wondered how much time there was
in the stale air of this ward, of used sanitary pans in the morning,
to think of the splendour of the breaking light at a dawn,
of the spirit newly risen.

Sour all day, I thought of Manickam, of my cousin's stories
of the stories of a friend,
a Chinese electrician. Once he had to defrost a public morgue -
his vivid phrase - how it stank to high heaven!

From Chairil Anwar (1922-1949)

i

Headstone
(For Grandmother)

It is not that death
has really found you out
but that you knew acceptance,
transcending all.
Out of the ashes and the pain
of your mortality
you are risen, sovereign
and boundless in your freedom.

ii
Spirit rampant

When the hour comes
there shall be
no redeeming word, no help,
not even from you.

Done with mourning,

I shall take on,
with all its unreason,
the blind unregeneracy
of the beast
forced in upon itself
and rage, though guns
may open great wounds in my sides,
rage against dying.

Bearing all wounds, all infections,
I shall press on

till past pain,
past mere mortality,
I seize an inward freedom,
will to live
yet another thousand years.

iii

At the mosque

I shouted to Him
till He came.

We clashed, bearing head-on,
face to face.

He glowed, a live flame
in the heart -
and would not be put out.

In great drops of sweat
I wrestled Him,
I would not
that I be broken to another's will.

In one single space,
in close confines,
I took my war to Him.

Seeking each the other
to annihilate,
one became consumed with curses,
the other, mad.

iv

I will have you back

If you should want it,
I will have you back -
with my whole heart.

I am yet alone.

You know you are not
as you have been before,
a flower others have looked at.

Do not look down.
Face me with your eyes, boldly.

If you should want it,
I will have you back -
wholly to myself.

Not even with the mirror
would I want you shared.

Garden

This is our garden,
garden that holds
you,
me
is room enough,
so small,
in it, one
will not lose
the other;
garden sufficient
to us
though the flowers
will not break out
in a multitude
of surprising colours,
and the grass
is not spread out
like a carpet
firm, yet soft
to the touch of feet.
This is for us
no great matter,
as, in our garden, garden that holds
you,
me,

you are the flower
and I, the bee
I am the bee
and, you, the flower.
Small and close, full of the mild sun,
this garden is place
sequestered,
far from the press,
far from the noise
of the common, intruding world.

As You Gently...

As you gently
bite me
on the mouth,
you touch off
hate; erupting,
it wells over.
Why did I not
strangle you, who
by your excess
of tenderness
cut into me
as into a wound?

Temple Caves

i

The opening winds down into the rock
bringing a short way light into massif of scarred stone
thrust up high out of the earth

to rest - mis-shapened, black against the sky
a severed head lying among the burnt out fields
with brow that abuts the sun.

Rising before the entrance, at the pond's end,
the sole mystical serpent grows large
with looking. It is faint shadow under the edge

diffused among the algae in water that glows
with the spreading chains of mucus, frog spawn
pushing for more life in the day's heat and moving air.

The seven heads branching, fanned out in full
distension of the hoods, the scales in rough lumps
and blunt, uneven fangs are set, made permanent,

so much of concrete the snake cannot turn back
upon its coils to weave out of the way of clouds
of midges, of dragonflies that swarm out of mere change

between the rains and these hot September days.

ii

The temple keepers bring to the darkness
thin fluorescent tubes as if to gain for the imagination
in one whitewashed chamber

ancestral images, guardians in such shapes
as mixture bonded of cement, crushed stone
and coarse river sand not wholly cleansed of mud would take.

Once they might have been presences.
Ranged round in their galleries, they now stand
disgorged from the deepest recesses of dream,

mere torsos, stiffened rib cages locked with wire
and heads hardened about bent pig-iron rods.
What can they suggest?

All that we can hope to know about being more
than merely human is held fast, mixed in with coarse grain
in bodies, calcified into substance

that daily becomes more solid, more resistant than stone.

iii

A ledge at the furthest end falls off...
A little way down by slow difficult descent
we lose the light.

Most are repelled by first scent of dung
which comes up sharply with body's heat
and, mixed into it, disquiet and the commotion we bring.

Once into the pit, we come up in darkness hard against
unyielding stone. It thrusts itself into the face and teeth
and, curving beyond the outstretched arms,

the fingertips on either side,
it beats back upon us our dis-ease.
So much of ourselves being of the senses, we gag for air.

The life we have stirred up here in this closed heat
is of our own. Inside ourselves we touch
hard wing and bone, a fearfulness, rage and hunger

that choke the mind, blind heave and swirl of bats
that clog its walls in boiling masses, in moving heaps,
dripping stalactites of blood and fur, of fighting claw and tooth.

We touch off a dream of fury that would not subside.

iv

After the first descent, we pass easily
into the stone. Where it opens, it leads us into uneven floors,
inward chambers, fissures, rock beds below which waters run.

In the moist air, where all sounds may be held,
resolved into the drawing in and flowing out of the breath
the senses dwindle, weaken

into a thin uncertain flame, without smoke,
clear on wick that burns and does not burn, detached
and floating at the still liquid centre of soft wax.

If we have lost the way now, what names,
what guides can we call upon? What bright presences
who will see us through? Out of the memory

of a life lived out in this our makeshift city,
out of the ways of a borrowed tongue and myth,
what can be retrieved, what word given which will make manifest

one who would lead us across echoing wells, ravines, black expanse of
    void?

v

Yet it has been rumoured there are exits
in the most unexpected places, sudden openings
in the rock widening outward to a milky darkness

lit by faint points of light aligned
in constellations not seen since long before
the first kings gave us laws,

taught us to make the most of water from the streams and sky,
to read into the future from markings on burnt shells
and, if it be given that there are hints,

once out into the open, one may look across
a bare terrain of random boulders, escarpments under water
and see in the distance the whole line of the sky

a forest, black and writhing under an ancient wind.
If it be given, the sun, now caught, will struggle
to tear and free itself from massed entanglement of coiled roots.

Breaking out of the earth, it will ascend
taking to itself half of the heavens, reveal itself
a tremendous bird of lightning, of the source of light,
bird that cleaves the world to itself in a consuming fire.

A Night Easter

i

Mariamma
(Night. Two women washing the body in the estate labour lines.)

How this room closes itself about your death;
the shock still hangs white upon the walls.
Horribly you set, the face kept taut over stiff bone,
and twisted into the cheek, a soft clay
where your fright and pain have died.
A second time your death has to come - I knew -
a second time. Only my heart is drawn tight
choked upon the strange dark fruit
of your body. The pent smoke
of the kitchen fires grows thick among the rafters
that cross the blackness beneath the roof.

>   *Gently, wash out gently, sand*
>   *from the gashes in his side.*

                              That day you came,
daylight was longer than we were used to
up these parts of the old estates. The crinum
burned like candles, throwing rich wax
upon the gravel driveway of the master's house.
When the moon was up...

>   *Soak clean the traces*
>   *of man's blood that cling about the bunched claw*
>   *of his hand.*

121

When the moon was up
there were noises as if the wind stirred
in the vegetation. Even then I knew your strangeness,
swaddled and dirty, a black unwanted child
with cow's eyes.

Your words have become confused, elusive
as our shadows grappling across the walls.
What changing shapes they make of two old crones!
And what stays is whitewash, concrete, squashed stains
of lice. Touching this coarse hair upon your arm
I cannot retain now what you meant,
and this mud caked about your soles,
what you meant about the kingdom.
But those who heard you knew your words
were real. I too knew they were real
as this flesh, and the malignant dreams
it harbours. I look down upon my shrivelled paps
and thighs, think of the pain that, some mornings,
hangs like a crab upon the groin, and ask
what is to be done?...
What is to be done?
Uselessly you died, just because
some stupid young girl loved you for your eyes.
I cannot weep but hold you embalmed
in my darkness. What then is there
That makes me wait? What is it that I have heard?
I cannot figure who there is who will move
this boulder, this heavy fleshiness from the heart.
this desolation that has crept into the flesh when now it withers.

ii

John 1

I had not known his word
could so afflict the flesh,
I had not known it could so take us,
strike us down into the ground,
that with our senses crushed, secreted
into its utter darkness, we could melt
into the compacted black grains
of the earth itself
and, in that sleep, not feel
the hand, that which made us,
slip past the opened ribs,
the congealed fountains of our blood
and probe our most secret places,
try us where no light has been.

Being but airless thick earth
of the body's night,
we purpose nothing - wait
till the great wounds close
and flesh
no longer feeds the fires
that wrap themselves about this body of the world,
till our senses dry into bone and tissue,
becoming fine scent

that breathes within the flesh.
Dying, the soul holds it fragrant,
sweet - holds it
as only a slightly
wrinkled, black and shining fruit.

Out of the body's night,
the soul's first desolation, a step
every which way is a step
returning...yet a step
past all dry places, all empty quarters,
white points of fire that cluster,
giving hints of sky, and winds
that still cry of distances
where the smell of grass and rivers
just begins...a step every which way
a going out...yet every which way
returning...a falling
into an abyss,
into true night, yet night that secures the soul.

iii

Manidas
(The labour lines. By lamplight, Manidas and another, a
visitor from the outside.)

The Other

And he said, *After the third week,*
out of the darkness I shall surely come again.
There is a darkness that I see here
that fans out at evening from the deep interior
of these estates. It catches from branch
to branch and, spreading like fine mist
from the trees, gathers and rises from the grass
and running water in snake-infested streams
and gullies to pour through thick banks of fern
to the ditch and roadway marking the estate's edge.
Your dogs whimper and howl at the black recesses,
at such forms the darkness engenders among the trees.

Mani

There was nothing of him in the charred teeth,
the brain pan splintered off his skull...
There was nothing of him that could have stirred again
out of the tremendous heat of that pyre.
He was sifted down into shadow, white upon grey wood ash.

The Other

But we have heard of signs. Of an evening,
when the crows made great tumult among the trees.

They moved in such a cloud, they surged
like a raging fire, black tongues of flame
leaping, subsiding along the tree line
that bends with that laterite road into the night.
The uproar swelled far into the hour
after an early moon was down.

Mani

His ashes left only a small trail of foam
quickly dispersed by the winds that rose among
the islands where we let him return into the sea.

The Other

But I have heard that the others... John...

Mani

John was silent afterwards for weeks.
He said only that he saw him. Muru also,
the evening he disappeared.

The Other

They say,
he did not come home, having gone to bathe
at the mining hole beyond the rail-track
where the foot trails peter out into lonely places.
It could have been the wind or a voice
blown across to him over the blackened waters.

Mani

It could only have been the wind...

The Other

The wind and, upon it rumours...traces of fur
pug marks - signs not seen here in these parts
for years.

Mani

Yes... Few would now work alone or come in late
from the outer reaches of these estates.
We put out early our cooking fires and keep
our windows shut. There is nothing out there
but a lighted brass lamp by that old tembusu
Its single yellow flame draws him, sets loose
upon itself all the darkness of the world.

The Other

It does seem
that you too believe. As if out of words alone...

Mani

Out of words alone we might well conjure
outside that door, in wait among the rafters,
and perhaps worse, leaning over your bed
in the small hours of the morning
as you start from sleep
what may now be out there ravening
among those wet and frightful recesses of trees.

The Other

And yet you say...

Mani

I say only
that there is much that we do not understand.
I do not know even what your calling is,
what signs that brought you out so far
to this district. There has been
no written word, no word of mouth.
Though gods and demons have been known
to find their way to us in dream
and, through it, becoming immanent in the word,
shine out to us as glittering jewel and fire,
out of all that beauty and all that terror,
we have been given nothing, nothing at all
that we could understand, that could warn us
of his coming. I would there were surer signs.
When these estates die, the frightful dreams
they breed will not survive the sun.
Out of the towns the new people come. Our ghosts
will not survive their new ways,
new intruding roads, new styles of speech...

Catch now this thick perfume. A hint of frangipani
drifts in from the lallang. You will not see
in this dark, that stretch of waste land at the back,
over-flowing, dripping thickly
from low trees in a somnolent, flowering grove.

John 2

During the first dreadful weeks, it seemed
a hand had stopped my ears. My tongue
was leather in my mouth. Then it came to me
while, working alone among the trees,
I would, over the next sharp rise of ground,
the stream's next turning, where the bird
started up from behind a dead tree stump, chance
upon that intense nothingness
breaking out into angry flame
over the dead leaves, among the brambles,
the same that out of which he came.

So it was...
returning from the stand of old trees
straggling far out into the rough foothills
one day, there was that other. I did not remark
upon his strangeness. He was more flame
than flesh. We did not speak.
After the rail-track crossing, I caught
the bitter smell of the smokehouses.
I found the gate into this compound.
Only in the darkness of this room I looked around.

He was the bright coal consumed in fire
within my heart, the melting walls,
spreading expanse of this compound,
the lallang waste, the flatlands of these estates
running into the hills. Over the ridges,
I heard the thunder of the darkness rolling in,
crashing into the sky, a boiling, black and devouring sea.

Postscript

Out of the Stony Rubbish
A Personal Perspective on the Writing of Verse in English in
Malaysia

If he gives any thought at all to writing as a vocation, the writer
in English in Malaysia very soon becomes painfully conscious of
a special kind of poverty that comes from being almost entirely
bereft of an identity that finds its confirmation in a community
of belief and tradition - and in the use of a received language
whose origins may be traced back to common ancestral
beginnings. This is particularly the case if he derives from any of
the immigrant communities that make up a large part of the
population of the country. The deprivation is not just in the
nature of breakdown and loss (a phenomenon characteristic of
twentieth century societies) of a pre-existing stable order but of
an absence, even at their very beginnings, of cultural and spiritual
resources carried over from a "mother" culture relevant to the
sustaining of a vital communal life in the new land. Without
access to a meaningful tradition or claim to even a disintegrating
one, the Malaysian writer in English brings, as it were, to his
work a naked and orphaned psyche.

In view of the very long histories and traditions of the lands
from which the immigrant peoples to Malaysia are drawn, it may
seem surprising that the communities which they make up
should provide almost nothing in their traditions for the cultural
and spiritual nourishment of their members. To explain this, it is
necessary to consider that the immigrant peoples did not arrive
in the country as communities such, for example, as the
Mayflower founding fathers, who consciously transplanted
themselves as a community to a new land in the cause of religious
freedom and brought intact with them as part of the fabric of the
life of the transplanted community a body of received beliefs and
tradition. Malaysians arrived mostly as individuals, infrequently
as families, up-rooted or forced out from their homelands by
war, famine, oppression or just simple poverty and want and,
most significantly, they were brought to the new land, as mere

factors of production. They were allowed in solely on the ground that they were useful and could contribute as productive factors to the economic life of enclaves established by the ruling colonial power in the new land. They were only means to further the economic and commercial ends of someone else. The communities that eventually developed out of the growing number of arrivals were thus not whole and intact vehicles for the extension of a "mother" culture carrying on and fostering a live tradition in a new land but a fortuitous coming together of individuals and families where accident of language and a commonality of geographical origins facilitate their casting in their lot together to further a common interest in survival.

The origins of the individuals and families which make up the immigrant communities ensured that even before their removal to the country of their eventual domicile they would come to the new settlements in a culturally (and spiritually) denuded state. By and large they belonged to the poorest of the poor classes in their homelands. My own antecedents, as were those of the majority among the Chinese, were at the outermost periphery of the then existing Chinese socio-economic order. The accretions of more than three millennia of history had left them unburdened of the ancient classics, of religious insight, of the Confucian prescripts for correct social relationships, of poetry and letters, the fine arts and so on. The inner guides to behaviour were a debased form of Taoism mixed with the veneration of ancestors and worship of household and other familiar spirits and a sense of kinship loyalty. These were the scant inheritance they brought with them to contend with the wilderness.

The wilderness provided soil for growth of a life whose interests extended little beyond the realm of the material - of things to be possessed. Such life as grew out of the inhospital soil was lived out for the purpose of maintaining the economic operations of the enclaves which as economic creations of the ruling power were informed by values which were not so much values as valuations of the market place, calculations of enterprise directed toward the technological exploitation of the environment for profit. The bare inheritance which the immigrant peoples brought with them was easily subverted by the new "values".

As purely economic ancillaries to the metropolitan centre of empire, the enclaves could not, by their very nature, have much else to offer. Though it might have been thought that the metrolitan power could be a source of an alternative inheritance, what it did in fact offer and what took root were little more than civic virtues of a humanitarian society, modern methods of organisation and administration necessary for maintaining the externalities of life of modern economic communities and ideas for creating the political framework for a later emergent independent state. The metropolitan power itself was part of a larger civilisation which had already gone far into the process of secularisation and consequent fragmentation and of the undermining of its traditional values and beliefs. Its heritage, which could no longer be easily taken for granted as a source of vital life by its own people, could not be appropriated by the enclave communities. Without that affinity of spirit that comes from a shared past, all the riches of the culture of the metropolitan power could not but be a heap of broken stones to the enclave communities - infinitely more so than to an Eliot contemplating the ruin of Western civilisation from the perspective of the nineteen-twenties.

Outside the enclaves, there were the older settled communities of the hinterland. As is usual with hinterland communities, agriculture was (and is) the basis of their economic life. In time, this was made over also into ancillary activities in support of the larger life of the enclaves. The hinterland supplied rice to these centres and grew a variety of cash crops, the principal one of which was rubber (now rivalled by oil palm) and the produce from these pursuits were sold to the centres for eventual export by agency houses to the metropolitan country. In becoming, in this way, economic ancillaries to the enclaves, these older settled communities which began as small riverine settlements in a new land, also experienced a change in their way of life. Apart from Islam, which served as an integrating factor, this way of life was also subverted by the new valuations of the market place. A large

135

part of the impact of this change was in men being drawn away by economic and other attractions to the enclaves. As Malay and, to a little extent, Arabic, taught in the religious schools, were the languages of these communities, they were not places out of which one would expect English writing to grow. As for the dispossessed persons in the enclaves, they were at that time not equipped, both linguistically and culturally, to attempt to write - not that writing was a priority in their lives anyway.

Though Malaysia has been officially declared a nation since 1957, the reality of its inner life is still that of the enclave. If anything, there has also grown into mature fruition by now out of the barren ground a pervading spirit of grasping individualism which encompasses a single-minded dedication to the pursuit of self-interest. This is invariably centred on the acquisition of possessions, status and power and consolidation of the means for their preservation. For the individual, all of the impulses toward a vital life are directed toward externalities such that the psyche is left unchecked to treat the world as object to be used in the fulfilment of its desires and to feed itself with its own dreams and fantasies about such fulfilment. Greed, anger, lust, and a "boastful pride of life" are thus given free rein. In the guise of progress and development, we have in consequence raised up idols of wealth, prestige and power and concupiscence whose worship is evidenced in the corruption, abuse of privilege and power, and lax sexual morality much rumoured about in public and business life. By the force of dedication to these gods, Malaysians have not been able to see the true wasteland that they inhabit among the stones of their high rise buildings, traffic fly-overs, bridges, dams, eight-lane highways, harbours and so on.

In such a wasteland, the realisation of a life enhancing vision through art by the writer will be almost, if not altogether, impossible to achieve. There cannot be the ambitions of a Yeats to reach back into folk tradition and myth to realise from their elements a transfiguring vision for a nation or even the failed attempts of a Hart Crane at creating a living myth to integrate the United States' vast, complex technological civilisation with a pre-Columbian past. In Malaysia, there are not available elements which an artist can draw together to create for the people an integrating vision of a possible inner life. What are available have so little power to move the spirit that they may more appropriately be seen as phenomenon for observation rather than elements for an integrating vision. Such observation involves reporting - a reporting of the pain, desolation and even horror of an inner state that has little possibility of mediation towards meaning, of the psyche being lost into itself to struggle in a morass created of itself of undirected feelings, fantasies, dreams and deeply buried unnameable primordial urges.

A strategy for rendering a true report on this inner state would be to find objects, places and situations in the external world as embodiment of the movements of the inner life. If there is to be a point to such "reporting", there must be implied norms as to what is the good ultimately in the life of a person and of a community. These are approached tangentially and implied in their absence in the inner life "reported" on. In my own practice, the implied norms, for instance, are those that would have served as sources of enlightenment or restraint on the behaviour which reveal the psychic lives of a number of relatives in the sequence "Remembering Grandma" or a "happier" inner state that could have prevailed in the place of a wasteland populated by dragons, snakes, pigs, dogs, bats, worms, tigers, even vegetation and such inert physical features of the landscape as bodies of water taking on the life of animals.

Though there is no explicit statement of such an inner state, there is, in the best of Malaysian poetry in English, in the work of Ee Tiang Hong and Shirley Lim a deep-seated unease that pervades the "reports" on the lives of men and women, in the relationships between themselves and others and between the individual and family, in the poets' psychological states, and even, as in Tiang Hong's work, the dissatisfactions with bureaucrats, institutions, official policies and so on. In his work, this comes out in the little ironies in such phrases as "men who mount" which appeared to have affronted the sensibilities of one or two people who, I had thought, would have been more perceptive. In the best work, there is also an absence of any inclination towards the definition of a "national consciousness" or aspirations towards the creation of a "Malaysian culture". There is no temptation to do any of these things unlike the situation in Singapore where even so astute a poet as Edwin Thumboo (a poet of sometimes the most exquisite lyricism) has not been entirely able to close his ears to the siren calls of "national purpose" but his response to the call is always complex and he is never guilty of uncritical assent to the official position. Ultimately, artistic work for the national cause, (at least this is made patently clear to writers in English in Malaysia), will be doomed to failure.

As irrelevant as writing for a "national purpose" would be is work which relies on a surface style that combines knowingness, mild irony and - polish, spiced with references to international events and personalities and work that passes itself off as "protest poetry", an infection caught by the practitioners very much in the out-dated fashion of the sixties during their carefree student days. The former avoids the real issues involved in artistic venture in Malaysia, indicating an unwillingness to pay the price of commitment the vocation demands, while the latter reveals a total and blissful blindness to how deep the darkness is in which we are plunged. The so-called protest poet in Malaysia is not a blind Tiresias who sees all. He only sees what he thinks are the "goodies" in the national product and questions the basis of the sharing of these "goodies" and thinks that by a mere redistribution of power and hence share of the GNP, he can hope to create a heaven on earth. While verse of the urbane and writing international style is still readable and at times entertaining, protest verse, at least in Malaysia, is always specious. The "poet" does not explore but begins with givens (provided by protest literature in the erstwhile colonial countries) on which he has already made his decisions and which he then attempts to "sell" to the reader. Like pornography, protest verse of the Malaysian kind is just another species of sentimentality.

A further option to the Malaysian wasteland is to opt out. This has most frequently been done by lapsing into silence. There are a few poets who have begun promisingly at university

138

but have not been heard from again. Cases in point are Lee Geok Lan and Pritam Kaur. Even those who continue writing do so in brief periods of activity with long years of silence in between. It would seem that the richness of feeling of each encounter with their daemon soon wears thin and the horror of the brute unadorned physicality of their existence shows through. The recourse in the face of such agony that surfaces is silence or emigration. Ee Tiang Hong and Shirley Lim are no longer with us (in a geographical sense, that is). Neither are Chin Woon Ping, T. Wignesan and Goh Poh Seng, all originally, I think, were Malaysians. In the Malaysian landscape, artists are, therefore, the maimed and the dead. Conditions do not make for the writing of poetry, let alone the hope of major poetry. There is no evidence of that yet - even in languages other than English. Barren ground is no ground for the attaining of transforming visions - a necessary though not necessarily sufficient condition for great poetry.

The way out of the desert seems to point towards the transcendent. It is a way that involves the finding and staying in touch with one's spirit. But this is not a way that an individual can carve out for himself on his own. He cannot invent his own myths or borrow them or go about in the modern manner of self-help to perform a variety of esoteric exercises to induce the sought for state. To be invested with authenticity, the individual has to submit himself to the disciplines and be guided by the beliefs of the great religions. This may be a way of liberation of man as artist up to a point. Beyond that point, we are always reminded of the choice between "perfection of the life" and "perfection of the work". But this could yet prove to be a fallacy. I believe that out of the transformation of life through seeking "perfection" there could come a kind of art that points beyond the wasteland. This will be the art of the man who has seen and comes back with a transformed vision of humanity - even perhaps of God in humanity. It will be an art of love, compassion and inward joy.

I am not sure that my contemporaries, Edwin and Tiang Hong, will agree or even approve of what I am going to say about language. However, I cannot evade the issue as I have always been exercised by the thought of my total dependence on English when I write. But I should say beforehand that, I do not subscribe to the myth of one having to imbibe a language together with one's mother's milk in order to be able, in a mysterious way, to use it with authority. In other words, I do not believe I am second best merely on account of the fact that there was only Cantonese in my mother's milk. I do believe that facility in a language is a matter of sensitivity and the capacity of the individual to internalise it together with its traditions - and therein lies the rub. To internalise a language is to allow it and the broad assumptions that the community of its native speakers hold about the universe to become a part of oneself. The non-English writer who writes in English and has no similar recourse to his own language is thus, in allowing English to take over his affective faculties, in a very deep sense a miscegenated being, very much and yet not an heir to the tradition of Shakespeare and Milton. The language he uses to name, organise and express his experience of the life around him removes him from that life and, whether he is aware of it or not, he becomes a stranger cut off and always looking in as an outsider into that life. In that sense, the more facility he has with the adopted language, the more unauthentic he becomes. Culturally and so, spiritually, he is induced to place himself in exile from England and be cast out of an imagined Eden. There is much irony in the older generation of Malaysian Chinese being "thrilled" at climbing the slopes of Mount Rydal or taking coffee at the London coffee house where Johnson used to hold court or be "at home" in London after Europe - something he would not say of Hong Kong or Taipeh.

I think it is this cultural displacement, more so than a matter of mother's milk, which makes it extraordinarily difficult for a Malaysian (or Singaporean) writing in English to achieve authentic life in poetry. It has always made me self-conscious about using English. To avoid inauthenticity in my own writing, I try to give primacy to immediate experience, to transform it into an internal event that assumes a sensory and emotional life of its own (much as in a dream) and then let it find outward expression through the mediation of words which are so organised as to give at the same time pointers to the possible meanings of the appropriated experience. The process may be described as involving a flooding out of English words with one's own immediate apprehension of the world to clean out their traditional English connotations whenever they intrude inappropriately into the texture and feel of the writing. To put it in another and very elementary way, it is the wiping away of "each soft incense that hangs upon the boughs" on a summer night or the colour and movement of daffodils from the word "flower" and putting in their place the rude, odourless and pendulous beauty of the hibiscus. The process of doing this is not a conscious one but is taken through by "feel" or a kind of instinct and in explaining it in the way I have done I might have even falsified it. However, in this way, if the genealogy of one's inner life is dominated by forebears with such strange sounding names as Mr Pope or Mr Wordsworth, one may contrive to appear as Malaysian as one possibly can.

Nevertheless, if the writer has to use the language, he has to treat it with respect and not do violence to its native genius. To achieve poetry, the use of words that make up the verse must give them resonance which comes from the emotive and intellectual associations acquired through the actual history of their usage. As the Imagists have shown, a purely physical poetry is limited in its possiblities. The Malaysian writer in English cannot avoid, despite what I have implied about the risks involved, falling in with the thought habits and conventions established in the native tradition of its usage. To maintain the tension arising between the demands of authenticity and genuine speech without the language breaking down altogether, the writer must then have a sense of occasion. He must know when to put the "thingness" of an experience into the words he uses and when to play this down and to allow for the connotations growing out of the tradition of the language to work and so give to the writing resonance. This sense of occasion comes out of and is guided by a sensitivity to words - individually, in phrases and in sentences - a sensitivity to their sound shapes, the sensory impressions they convey, their feel, their emotional and intellectual associations, and their etymology (particularly important in English which, because of its hybrid Norman French-Anglo-Saxon character has a very wide "tonal" and "colour" range to be exploited to great effect). A sense of occasion is also relevant in a consideration of verse form and metre, though for the Malaysian writer in English the options available amounts to little more than an eschewing of traditional forms and metres. Strict form is too much a part of the English tradition to be easily carried over into Malaysian writing. Since the only tradition and cultural achievements that our Malaysian forebears can lay claim to do not go beyond rice fields, river house-boats, small shops, artisan's workshops, servants' quarters, labour lines and so on, English verse forms, which are an expression of a long tradition of Western letters and scholarships whose sources of inspiration go back to the ancient Greek and Latin classics, cannot be easily appropriated by Malaysian writers to serve their own totally different ends. However one would read it, a Shakespearean or Miltonic sonnet written in Malaysia would be too artificial a device to ring true. Malaysian poets, (I hope I am not pontificating here) cannot afford to risk more than writing fourteen-line stanzas, which through the organisation of the argument in eight and six line segments or three four-line segments with a concluding line pair merely suggest the form of a sonnet. This, together with un-rhymed three-liners, suggesting the terza rima, and other pieces using verse paragraphs with a fixed number of unrhymed lines appear to be the most feasible approach to form for the Malaysian writer. For lack of an old hinterland steeped in a feudal/rural culture that has continuity with our present situation, even the ballad in however vaguely suggested a form, will not work in the Malaysian wasteland.

As is the instance of verse form, traditional English metre is very much of an inheritance from the classical literatures of Greece and Rome. In the very best practice, however, there is a freedom with which English poets handle prosody allowing the rhythms of the native speech to break out of the strict confines of rules derived from the practice in languages in which the measure of a metrical foot is counted by vowel lengths rather than by stresses. Here the Malaysian writer finds authority in the English tradition itself to follow natural speech rhythm and the sound shape of the words he uses in constructing his lines rather than worry over much about counting feet. As Malaysian practice would not be different from practice elsewhere in the world where English verse is written, there is no need here to deal at greater length with the matter.

An external aspect of the Malaysian poetic wasteland is the lack of, for want of a better word, an infrastructure for the support of its propagation and growth. There are almost no opportunities for publishing, no audience (except for isolated individual readers here and there), no forum for critical discussion and certainly no official encouragement of good work through the giving of awards and so on. The official attitude on the teaching of English is based on the belief that learning and mastering of a language can be achieved even if it is severed, nerve and artery from the body of the literature and culture in which it thrives and finds continuing life. Writers in English are

left very much alone, though in a recent anthology of Malaysian English verse in translation into Bahasa Malaysia, there is some small acknowledgement of the existence of serious writing in languages other than Bahasa Malaysia. The cavalier fashion in which the English is translated, however, raises doubt as to whether the best interests of the writers have been served. In the instance of my own verse, "started" in the sense of a sudden movement or a sudden waking up from a reverie has been rendered as "bermula" which is the Bahasa for "commencing" or "beginning" while the glass panel on my step-mother's coffin becomes, in the translator's eyes, "cermin mata" or spectacles.

The critical question for the Malaysian writer in English is one of audience. To whom does he address himself? Largely to the dead in Baudelaire's sense of the unborn. To say this is to risk appearing to make large and pretentious claims. Yet, the claims reside only in the hope that what is written will be read some time into the future - the hope that here and there in the present and in the future there will be those who are interested in

Malaysian writers as witnesses to a time and place and what has been identified, named and brought to outward expression as the psychic/spiritual contours of their inner landscape and such "truths" as they may happen on about the human condition. This hope is surely the motivation of the Malaysian writer for lack of a direct living audience and if he fails in its realisation, his only consolation is that he would not be around to endure the pangs of his disappointment. As a last word, I will say only that should Malaysian serious writing in English survive, it will not be so much Malaysian writing as a part of Malayan-Singapore writing if only on the ground that, for poetry at least, we have common beginnings in the late 1940's in the University of Malaya in Singapore. This is despite the tendency of the younger Singapore writers to go their way to construct a Singapore "national" literature albeit it will largely be in English. For Malaysians our hope is that writers, poets in particular, will not conveniently die out like dinosaurs.

'MAKING ONE'S LANGUAGE AS ONE GOES ALONG: WONG PHUI NAM'S "WAYS OF EXILE"'

By

PROFESSOR ALAN DURANT

(School of English, Cultural & Communication Studies,
Middlesex University, London)

In his foreword to this collection, K.S. Maniam draws attention to how Wong Phui Nam ended his own Introduction to the first edition of 'How the Hills are Distant' in the 1960s with an especially suggestive remark about the central role played in his work by a *creative* use of poetic language:

> On looking back I realise I have written these poems for those who truly understand what it means to have to make one's own language as one goes along. [1]

In a precise sense, of course, the situation Wong alludes to is rarely literally true. Language is almost by definition something which pre-exists the individual user; and so 'making one's own language as one goes along' - no matter how extensive the process may seem to someone engaged in it - it almost always a process of only marginal modifications, revision or coinage. Essentially conventional and social characteristics are what most clearly distinguish a genuinely living language from a made-up, personal or private 'language'. In this sense, Wong's English (as he recognized when he indicates that he is, at least partly, an 'heir to the tradition of Shakespeare and Milton' [2] is in important ways an already-established - if nonetheless problematic - social and historical construct.

In a less literal sense, however, Wong Phui Nam's statement signals an important dimension of the poet's work. Writing poetry not only draws on existing linguistic and cultural codes, but also transforms given materials so that they can articulate, in a texture of often unresolved connections, new and unique perceptions and social experience. In the case of English writing in Malaysia, this individually creative, rather than conventional or formulaic aspect of poetic writing is amplified by two specific factors. The multilingual situation of the country, in which English occupies a marginal and unstable position alongside Malay, Chinese, Tamil and other languages, means that writing in English already represents a very significant choice - a choice made all the more problematic by a current divergence, in attitudes towards English, between traditions carried over from its earlier colonial imposition on the one hand, and its siren, contemporary role as threshold to an international world of technology and commerce on the other. Writing in English in Malaysia in these circumstances represents a marked cultural choice - a choice no doubt overdetermined by responses to a range of issues concerning personal and national identity, foreseen local and foreign readerships, and attitudes towards culture and colonialism.

Having selected English as the preferred medium of public expression, at a practical level the Malaysian poet is obliged to mould existing usage of the language to the task of describing emotional attitudes, thought processes and experience for which its history has not directly suited it. The scale of this task - and accomplishment in it - would be self-evident, if 'making one's own language as one goes along' were achieved through neologism, dense use of dialect markers or thickness of local cultural allusion; but the achievement is equivalent even where newness lies in nuance, in implied connections between concepts or images, or in local rhythmic patterns or speech conventions. Commenting on such formal aspects of his work, Wong Phui Nam describes what he sees as a need to 'clean out' words of their traditional English connotations whenever these intrude into the texture of the writing, and so to forge new possibilities for them. [3] It is in this sense - of subtle nuance, as English is redirected towards new, specifically Malaysian purposes - that the poetry in this collection constitutes, beyond its clear importance within the national literature of Malaysia, a significant innovation within English expression internationally, and occupies an important (and unduly neglected) position within the emergent New Literatures in English.

II

In order to appreciate the urgency with which Wong Phui Nam's poetry tackles the question of a newly-made language, however, we should consider further the sense of necessity conveyed by the words 'have to' in Wong's formulation. What is it he assumes is lacking? As Wong puts it in the brief reflective essay, 'Out of the Stony Rubbish' (included in this volume), there is for the Malaysian poet writing in English no common body of cultural assumptions or traditions on which to draw. The poet writing in English in Malaysia, he argues, therefore 'becomes painfully conscious of a special kind of poverty that comes from being almost entirely bereft of an identity that finds its confirmation in a community of belief and tradition - and in the use of a received language whose origins may be traced back to common ancestral beginnings.'[4] Emphasising further the deprivation he considers a consequence of this situation, Wong continues, 'Without access to a meaningful tradition or claim to even a disintegrating one, the Malaysian writer in English brings, as it were, to his work a naked and orphaned psyche.'[5]

The circumstances Wong Phui Nam alludes to here are specific and historical, rather than permanent or essential; they form part of the colonial, and more recently postcolonial, history of Malaysia rather than a general South East

Asian or even Third World artistic consciousness or sensibility. At the time of Wong's early writing, in the late 1950s, Malaysia was entering a major phase in its shift - during a period of rapid global decolonisation - from colonial rule towards government by an emergent Malay ruling class, following the defeat of revolutionary communist forces. What is significant about this period as regards writing in particular is that by this time earlier, colonial literary aspirations were already largely discredited (partly as a result of arguments taking place elsewhere about Indian and African writing in English), but new directions for Commonwealth Literature which were gradually being defined in a number of post-colonial situations were as yet not being self-confidently or accessibly promulgated in Malaysia itself.

As part of a generation of Chinese Malaysians born in the 1930s, Wong came to maturity and studied at a university with a marked European cultural bias at the end of the 1950s, within an active, indigenous intellectual culture whose links to arguments being debated by intelligentsias in other, comparable situations were nevertheless restricted by political conditions. It is true that, following its establishment in Singapore at the end of the 1940s, the University of Malaya acted as a centre for literary discussion and composition. But the influence of the so-called 'Pioneer poets' (Lim Thean Soo, Beda Lim, Goh Sin Tub) had passed its immediate peak, and the work of writers such as Muhammad Haji Salleh, Omar Mohd, Pretam Kaur and Shirley Geok-lin Lim was still to come. Bridging the divide between colonized and post colonial formations - and paving the way for this later generation of writers - the 'university poets' (Edwin Thumboo, Wong and Ee Tiang Hong, first gathered together in the collection Litmus One: Selected University Verse, 1949-1957) experimented to an unprecedented degree, while remaining in some ways within a formative, Western literary-cultural paradigm shaped by Modernist writers such as T.S. Eliot. [6]

In the context of these broad circumstances and influences, the sense Wong Phui Nam forms during this period of what he calls a 'cultural wasteland' takes on a clearer shape. But that sense has several further, interlocking historical causes which are also worth noting.

First, there is the much earlier formation in Malaysia of a Chinese diaspora, following extensive but piecemeal immigration. Wong himself reports that the Chinese migrants from whom he is descended were deprived, by class position, from access to much of the Chinese culture they otherwise might have brought with them; and since they arrived in small groups rather than as a single community (unified as colonisers, soldiers, or evangelists, for instance) they could not easily establish a common set of roots from which later cultural forms might grow in any kind of continuous descent.

Second, a high degree of cultural separation between Malays, Chinese and Indians has retarded in Malaysia the process of formation of a new, common (and necessarily hybrid) cultural tradition which might have been expected to result from extensive social contact and intermarriage between communities, and from multilingualism and translation between languages. Such ethnic, cultural and religious separation, which has occasionally fuelled mutual suspicion between the respective communities, has inhibited the emergence of a distinctively new syntax of Malaysian multicultural identity that might be reflected in literary and other forms.

Third, as regards English in particular, language policies since Independence (unlike those adopted by many other formerly colonized, Anglophone countries) have resulted in a lack of institutions or outlets for writing; and more generally, Wong notes, one 'external aspect of the Malaysian poetic wasteland is the lack of, for want of a better word, an infratructure for the support of its propagation and growth'. [7] Nationalist reaction against English in the 1960s and 1970s significantly reduced the potential national audience for English writing, and appears to have implied on some occasions that English writing involves a form of cultural dissent.

Fourthly, and relatedly, relative isolation of individual writers from one another has resulted in a shortage of opportunities for discussion or for informal critical comment and review. Contemplating this isolation, Wong has said that the Malaysian writer accordingly as 'much in the situation of, perhaps, the mythical shipwrecked sailor who casts messages in sealed bottles into the sea, relegating them to the wind and tide to carry themselves wherever they ill.'

Considered together, these four factors produce for Malaysian writing in English a distinctive dynamic within the global development of post-colonial literatures. The unique configuration of ethnic, economic, religious and other factors should, of course, preclude generalized response to Malaysian writing as being somehow representative of 'Third World literature' (eg. on the basis of an assumption that individual works should be consistently read as 'allegories of national experience' [8], and so should guarantee an international hearing for works by Wong Phui Nam and other important Malaysian writers. At the same time, however, to the extent that little of the writing in English produced in Malaysia has dealt with cultural or political struggle, or been aligned with perceived socially progressive forces within the society - the two main factors which typically recommend non-European writing to the attentions of a metropolitan Western readership - Malaysian writing remains neglected by comparison with works from (for example) the Philippines, the Indian sub continent, or Southern Africa. For his part, nevertheless, Wong dismisses politically partisan writing, on the basis that,

> Ultimately, artistic work for the national cause (at least this is made patently clear to writers in English in Malaysia) will be doomed to failure. [9]

III

If we are to read Wong Phui Nam's poetry closely, within these larger coordinates of the changing literary geography of English, it is important briefly to consider two consequences described above, as regards what Wong chooses to write about and how his writing is presented: first, the generic or formal conventions Wong chooses to follow; and second, what might be called the poetry's patterns of repetition, contrast and transformation between themes and topics.

The collection 'Ways of Exile' is made up of four sections, each a sequence of short lyrics: 'How the Hills are Distant', in which 'Nocturnes and Bagatelles' convey a sense of loneliness and separation accentuated for the poet by being awake during the night; 'For a Local Osiris', which depicts a resurrected, mythical Osiris seeking to redeem an evil world for civilization; 'What are the Roots...', which contains English version of Taoist poems and writings by Tu Fu, evidently as a quest to constitute or restore an absent poetic tradition; and 'Rumours of Exits', which presents a range of images of death, as well as modes of access to a transcendental, other world. [10]

Throughout, these sequences reflect in their modes of composition a set of constraints Wong feels exist on writing English poetry in Malaysia. For example, he discusses difficulties presented by certain English verse forms, such as the sonnet or ballad, arguing that these appear inappropriate to a culture with a largely agrarian history; Wong prefers short lyrical forms arranged in loose sequences to such closely-structured idioms. Noting, too, the suggestiveness of precise details of register, Wong negotiates issues of mode of address and sense of occasion by opting for an introspective lyrical subjectivity rather than any suggestion of public declaration. And in 'What are the Roots...', translation plays an important role in creating a specifically Chinese Malaysian poetic voice. Rejecting the idea of scholarly, word-for-word

151

translation, as well as such terms as 'imitations' or 'interpretations', Wong argues rather that, 'Because of the differences between the languages, I feel the best strategy for rendering an English version of a Chinese text is to write it as if it is an original poem in English' [11]; and pointing to the cultural purpose of translation - perhaps especially resonant in the Tu Fu sequence - he suggests that translation makes possible 'putting poems into English, and saying, in the process, something about the Malaysian condition in ways I could not manage in my own verse'. [12]

It is less, however, this ability of translation to symbolise contemporary cultural conditions than more local symbolic patterns which has given rise to descriptions of Wong Phui Nam's work as especially rich in symbolic qualities. Much of his reputation follows from the observation that a focus for many of the poems is provided by two recurrent symbols - the body and the landscape - woven together into a symbolic texture which is well illustrated by the following lines from poem (vi) in the 'Hills' sequence:

> I feel out of the verges of the swamps
> in the body's tides, out of the bones
> of an ancient misery,
> the dead stir with this advent of rain;
> and in a landscape too long
> in the contours of a personal anguish,
> assume its presences: hedges and barb-wire,
> trees in the numbness of the field;
> and, moving in the dark between the houses,
> conjure the heart
> to breed upon the hint of a primal terror. [13]

In other poems in the sequence (where more conventional contrasts are also drawn between city corruption and escape into the natural world), landscape is presented in an extension from established pastoral conventions as a representation simultaneously of physical, mental and social structure; and Wong depicts the death of the individual, anatomically and graphically, both to record individual pain and to symbolise more general forms of cultural death (perhaps most effectively in the poem 'For my old amah'). Working through patterns of symbolic equivalence, contrast and transformation, Wong develops personal, contemplative lyrics into larger-scale, social and philosophical comment.

But if such descriptions suggest that 'Ways of Exile' is concerned only with decay, pain, and death, it should be emphasised that a way out of 'the desert', and out of 'primal terror', lies for Wong in what he calls the 'transcendent' [14]. A symbolic pattern suggestive of this 'transcendent' presence is developed, for example, in Wong's translation 'A Mountain Visit', where the poet's efforts and labour in ascent (searching, significantly, for 'an ancient trail') are contrasted with the tranquility, plenitude and knowledge offered on arrival by the poet's conversation with a figure ('the master') whom the poet has clambered up to consult. Here are the opening lines:

> The mountains here dissolve into the one blue
> of the sky - into silence - towards a stillness
> beyond the bounds of time. I grope my way up them
> through descending banks of cloud, feel
> for traces of an ancient trail.

But the temporary stasis and plenitude enjoyed by the poet is quickly displaced; and the poem ends with the poet symbolically returned to his 'ways of exile':

> I find the master in. Our conversation fades
> with the light which turns rivers into slow veins
> blackening on the far plains at the approach of night.
>   Alone, I stumble my way down into biting cold and
>   fog. [15]

In citing the title of the collection here, however, we should pause to consider what 'exile' means in this context. The term has gained such currency in recent cultural analysis that its meanings are complex, ranging from a literal sense of political expulsion to figurative description of a universal, ontological condition of general 'uprootedness' [16]; and a convergence between these two senses - brought about partly by intellectuals from post-colonial countries now resident in the West, and combining in some instances political engagement with post-structuralist theory - has helped in efforts to include New Literatures within university and school curricula. Wong's own use of the term - unlike Ee Tiang Hong, Wong has continued to live in Malaysia - brings together a sense of present cultural marginalisation with a more abstract sense of historical displacement influenced (like many writers and teachers of the period) by T.S. Eliot's belief in the essential value of cultural tradition. Set alongside the palliative of transcendent forces invoked in Wong's poetry, 'exile' also implies exclusion from a paradise which cultural belonging might have provided.

Wong's most interesting insights combine the influence from Eliot, however, with acute observations about the situation of the Malaysian writer, as in this striking passage from the 'Stony Rubbish' essay, which is worth quoting at length:

> The non-English writer who writes in English and has no similar recourse to his own language is thus, in allowing English to take over his affective faculties, in a very deep sense a miscegenated being, very much and yet not an heir to the tradition of Shakespeare and Milton. The language he uses to name, organise and express his experience of the life around him removes him from that life and, whether he is aware of it or not, he becomes a stranger cut off and always looking in as an outsider into

that life. In that sense, the more facility he has with the adopted language, the more unauthentic he becomes. Culturally, and so spiritually, he is induced to place himself in exile from England and be cast out of an imagined Eden. [17]

The parallels with Eliot are evident, stylistically as well as conceptually (for example, in such words and phrases as 'heir to the tradition' and 'unauthentic', or in the essay title itself, 'Out of the Stony Rubbish' - as elsewhere in Wong's idea of a 'cultural wasteland', the 'impossibility of meaning', or the 'primal terror'). But the argument has gained a vital new dimension, by focusing on how the cultural incongruity of the colonial language interrupts perceptions which might connect the poet more closely with his or her immediate social surroundings, while, implicitly, a combination of Malay hegemony and the earlier, intellectual formation of the poet block off the otherwise obvious nationalist, vernacular alternatives.

It is this cluster of concerns with language and social belonging which most distinguish and inspire Wong Phui Nam's writing; at the same time, forms of repetition or closure in the treatment of these concerns signify the formative conditions of his work. Wong's term 'miscegenation', for instance, has increasingly been re-cast in post-colonial writing as a phenomenon of 'cultural hybrid-sation' (in which experimentation in local or 'nativized' dialects of English plays an important part [18]; and much contemporary argument over post-colonial literatures takes *as one of its starting-points* a presumption that English is no longer the property of native speakers, given a shifting global balance between monolingual and bilingual uses of the language. Despite risks of being lumped together in a simplistic unity of 'oppositionality' and otherness - especially in the hands of Western reviewers and critics - post-colonial writers and critics have increasingly explored comparisons between respective national experiences, and developed supportive connections with each other (including with writers literally in exile).

Such descriptions can easily seem idealistic or pious, however; and Wong Phui Nam himself remained silent through the 1970s and most of the 1980s, returning to public prominence again with 'Remembering Grandma and other Rumours' in 1989. Rather than contributing to a global dialogue ironically facilitated by the colonial imposition of English, in fact, contemporary Malaysian writing in English may merely 'die out like dinosaurs' (as Wong himself suggests [19]). But if this happens, then readers and writers alike will have failed fully to appreciate the insights into linguistic and cultural identity presented so vividly in this collection of Wong Phui Nam's work.

NOTES

1. See above (this collection), p. 3.
2. p. 140.
3. p. 141.
4. p. 133.
5. p. 133.
6. For more detailed discussion, see, Anne Brewster, 'The Sense of place in Singaporean and Malaysian poetry in English with special reference to Wong Phui Nam and Arthur Yap', in Peggy Nightingale (ed), *A Sense of Place in the New Literatures in English* (St. Lucia: University of Queensland Press, 1986), pp. 132-42. For a longer critical history of writing in English in Malaysia, see, Lloyd Fernando, *Cultures in Conflict: Essays on Literature and the English Language in South East Asia*, esp. pp. 128-49.
7. p. 143..
8. For a detailed argument along these lines, see, Fredric Jameson, 'Third World LIterature in the Era of Multinational Capital', *Social* Text, Fall (1986), 65-88. A range of perspectives on the degree of generalization, based on 'common denominators', that is reasonable with regard to

regional or otherwise marginal 'minority' discourses can be found in Abdul R. Janmohamed and David Lloyd (eds), *The Nature and Context of Minority Discourse* (Oxford: OUP, 1990).

9. p. 138.
10. For further commentary, see Anne Brewster, op. cit.
11. p. 87.
12. p. 86.
13. p. 11.
14. p. 139.
15. p. 84.
16. For an exemplary discussion of the development of post-colonial literatures (and reactions to them) which investigates in detail relationship between writing, intellectuals, and political circumstances, see Aljaz Ahmad, *In Theory: Classes, Nations, Literatures* (London: Verso, 1992).
17. p. 140.
18. For discussion of creative uses of English in New Literatures in English, see, for example, Braj Kachru, *The Other Tongue: English Across Cultures* (Oxford: Pergamon Press, 1982); and for more general background to the emergence of the New Englishes, see, John Pride, *New Englishes* (Rowley, Mass: Newbury House, 1982), or Robert McCrum, William Cran and Robert MacNeil, *The Story of English* (London: Faber, 1986). Some relevant theoretical perspectives are offered in, Chinweizu, Ouwuchekwa Jemie and Ihechukwu Madubuike, *Toward the Decolonization of African Literature: African fiction and poetry and their critics* (London: KPI, 1980); Randolph Quirk and H.G. Widdowson (eds), *English in the World: teaching and learning the language and Literatures* (Cambridge: CUP, 1985); Homi Bhabha (ed), *Nation and Narration* (London: Routledge, 1990); Gayatri Chakravorty Spivak, *The Post-colonial Critic: Interviews, Strategies, Dialogues* (London: Routledge, 1990); and Edward W. Said, *Culture and Imperialism* (London: Chatto and Windus, 1993).
19. p. 144.

Skoob *PACIFICA* Anthology No: 1
S. E. ASIA WRITES BACK !
Publication date: 31st Aug. 1993, P'bk. U.K. Price GBP £5.99

As the advancement of technology exceed our grasp, contemporary culture has reached the juncture between Postmodernism and Postcolonialism to give rise to an entirely new idea of chronology. The 'Post' is a diachrony of periods which are individually identifiable. This is the point where we begin. The principle of Postmodern/Postcolonial writing is to deviate from the tradition and to develop a new direction of thought. Such an idea of progress would lead to the evolution of culture. The understanding of a writer involves anamnesis in psycho-analytical context, the free association of ideas and imagery of the unconscious in situations past to discover the hidden meanings of his life.

The Postmodern/Postcolonial writer is in the position of a philosopher: the text written is not, in principle, governed by predetermined rules nor is it judged according to a determining judgement. Those rules and categories are what the work of art is defining. The writer is working without rules in order to formulate the rules of what "will have been done". Hence, the text has a character of the event which comes too late for the author, it's *mise en oeuvre* is ahead of itself. This could be understood according to the paradox of the future (post) anterior (modo). The achievement of the Postcolonial writers is that they see within the self the possibility of a different history, and stemming from this, the reality of a new *genre*.

Preface by I.K. Ong
Introduction by John McRae
PART ONE: New Writings
Shirley Geok-lin Lim * K.H. Thor * Karim Raslan * Robert Yeo *
Arthur Yap * Philip Jeyaretnam * Alfred A. Yuson * Michael Wilding *
Jan Kemp * W.P. Chin * Paul Sharrad * K.S. Maniam * Latiff Mohidin *
Cecil Rajendra * L.G. Leong * T.P. Lee * Kirpal Singh * Anne Brewster *
Siew-Yue Killingley * P.N. Wong
PART TWO: Malaysian/Singaporean Prose in English
Shirley Geok-lin Lim * K.S. Maniam * K.L. Lee * C.W. Watson *
B.E. Ooi * T.C. Kee
PART THREE: Other Literatures of the Pacific Rim
Marcus Richards * Pira Sudham * P.N. Wong * Alan Durant
PART FOUR: The Nobel Laureates
Derek Walcott * Wole Soyinka * Yasunari Kawabata
PART FIVE: Literary Features
Yukio Mishima - Fountains In The Rain
Vikram Seth - From Heaven Lake, Travel Through Sinkiang And Tibet

K.S. MANIAM
The Return
Now Available, P'bk. U.K. Price GBP £5.99

It is a time of both apprehension and hope. The youthful narrator, Ravi witnesses the change in a way of life and the end of a way of thinking. The story depicts the experiences of an immigrant community in Peninsula Malaysia before and after Independence in 1957. It documents the bewilderment and loss of bearings felt within a once secure world coming to an end in political change and cultural fragmentation.

"HOW DOES ONE DESCRIBE THE LAND ONE LIVED IN BUT NEVER SAW? It was more tangible than the concrete one we flitted through every day. Darkness gave it true dimensions. Then it vibrated within our hearts. If we saw, perhaps through some quirk of optics, a flame beside the drain, then it was a dead pregnant woman's soul come out to haunt the real world; if we heard murmurs, echoed voices among the hills, they were the chanting and tinkling of Banana-tree spirits dancing in the courtyard of the night. The quick rush of water in the communal bath-shed signified some unappeased soul's feverish bathing. We were hemmed in our rooms, houses, and in our minds. The tension between good and evil shimmered therefore like an inevitable consciousness within our heads."

K.S. Maniam, *The Return*

K.S. Maniam is a myth-maker, reconciling Malaysian and ethnic Indian consciousness in an organic symbolism rooted in unconscious experience.

The growing reputation of *The Return* is much deserved, and in its appearance in this new edition will allow new readers a rare opportunity to enter imaginatively into a certain kind of Malaysian experience which is paradoxically perhaps, both highly specific and yet universally representative.

Dr. C.W. Watson, *University of Kent at Canterbury*

Maniam was already known as a writer of some fine short stories, and his first novel lived up to our expectations. The Style was impressive, creating and sustaining, seemingly without effort...

This second edition of *The Return* should win it many new readers and, hopefully, raise a crop of novelists in English, settlers moving in to cultivate new terrain, inspired by Maniam's worthy pioneer achievement.

Edward Dorall, *New Straits Times*

K.S. MANIAM
In A Far Country
The New Novel
Now Available, 1993, P'bk. U.K. Price GBP £5.99

The protagonist, Rajan, disillusioned with the trappings of silk and satin, reflects on his unrelenting past and old companions. In trying to recant a persona of attachment to material progress, he discovers self-apprehension in an authentic identity.

What was he? The question obsessed me for a long time. But as I went on watching I understood only a little of what he was and wanted to be...

Lee Shin seems to have come to the settlement with a fierce desire to safe-guard his freedom. From the beginning he has kept to himself as if he mistrusted people...

Sometimes his movements are so painfully slow that the observer wonders if Lee Shin has entered some sort of a trance. There he stands, within an invisible centre, his body defying gravity...

Then Lee Shin puts the shiny object to his lips and the sound it emits confuses the observer for a while and then only amuses him. As he launches into a full melody, the observer becomes more and more disoriented...

As the days pass, Lee Shin plays furiously but stops now and then to look in the direction of the observer's house. In the company's offices he casts shy but significant glances at the observer. Is some change imminent in Lee Shin?...

Some weekends Lee Shin tramps off into the jungle nearby, haversack on his back and a butterfly net in his hand. Returning in the evening, he sits in the hall and mounts the specimens. The observer sees him bent over the butterflies, the syringe in his fingers sucking out the insides and, later, pumping in the formaldehyde. What is there about the posture that says neither the activity nor the interest will last?...

The observer mounts the steps and stands beside Lee Shin. The man makes no move to acknowledge or greet him. Lee Shin's gaze is still turned towards the house down the slope as if the observer has not left it. Then, suddenly, he snaps out of his reverie and looks at the observer.

"The harmonica music has brought you here," Lee Shin says.

"In a way," I say.

The power and necessity to tell a story is the original impulse of any fiction. Rajan, Zulkifli, Lee Shin, Sivasurian and Santhi of different race and religion contribute to the cosmos of this convergent world In A Far Country.